Life on the E

Judy Horacek is a well-known Australian cartoonist and writer who has been widely published both in Australia and overseas. Her cartoons are found on fridges and toilet doors throughout the world and her work has appeared in *The Australian*, *The Age*, *The Sydney Morning Herald* and numerous magazines, journals and books. Major exhibitions of her work have been held at the National Gallery of Victoria, (*Laughter, the Universe and Everything*, March 1999, then toured Victoria until 2001) and the National Museum of Australia, (*I am woman hear me draw* in 2002, now touring nationally). Six collections of her work have been published. Horacek cartoons appear on greeting cards, tea-towels, T-shirts, aprons, mugs and fridge magnets. Judy also makes limited edition prints, and runs a website full of cartoons at www.horacek.com.au

Other books by Judy Horacek

UNREQUITED LOVE (1994)
WOMAN WITH ALTITUDE (1997, 1998)
LOST IN SPACE (1998)
IF THE FRUIT FITS (1999)
I AM WOMAN, HEAR ME DRAW (2002)

Life on the Edge

cartoons by Judy Horacek

introduced by Dale Spender

SPINIFEX

Spinifex Press Pty Ltd,
504 Queensberry Street,
North Melbourne, Vic. 3051
Australia

First published by Spinifex Press, 1992
Reprinted 2003

Typeset in Goudy by Claire Warren, Melbourne
Made and printed in Australia by McPherson's Printing Group

CIP
Horacek, Judy, 1961–
    Life on the edge : cartoons.

    ISBN 1 876756 41 1

    1. Women – Social conditions – Caricatures and cartoons.
    2. Minorities – Social conditions – Caricatures and cartoons.
    3. Australian wit and humour, Pictorial. I. Title.

741.5994

To Mum, Dad, Michael, Francis and Peter.
A huge thanks to everyone who has ever supported
my cartoons and all those who helped with this book.

Introduction

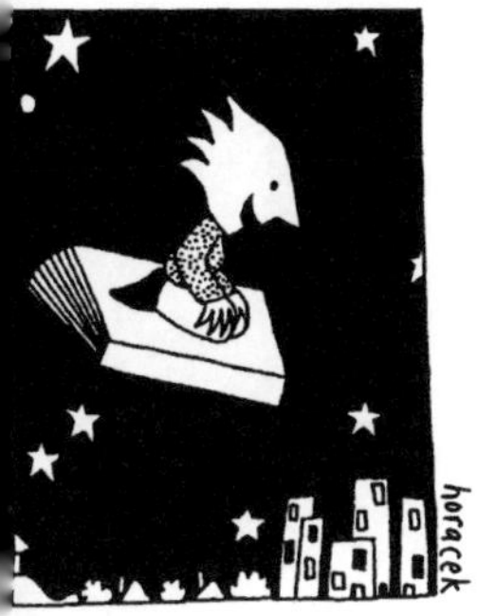
horacek

The issue of women and humour has to be the starting point for an introduction to a volume of cartoons – by a woman. This is because we expect cartoons to be insightful, funny, comic, humorous. Yet the conventional wisdom of a male dominated society has been that women have no sense of humour – therefore they cannot be expected to create comic – or cutting – cartoons.

Indeed, so pervasive has been the premise of women's absence of humour, that any suggestion that women can be funny, witty, splendidly subversive or satirical, has itself come to be something of a joke.

This is why it is almost impossible to talk about the success and significance of women's cartoons without reference to the values of the society which gives rise to them. For those who are allowed to be humorous, – to quip, tell jokes, mock, make fun of, and caricature etc. – have access to a considerable source of social control and power. And it is no accident that it has been men who have enjoyed the right to be the humour makers. Nor is it an accident that women have been defined as the individuals who have no sense of humour, and whose role it is to serve as the butt of the joke.

When it comes to humour, women have routinely been warned off. They have been informed that they cannot be funny, and what is more, they shouldn't even try. Which is why the emergence of women's humour – and of feminist cartoons – is much more than an additional form of entertainment. It represents a fundamental shift in power.

Judy Horacek's work, along with that of many other feminist humorists, or *fumerists*,[1] is a serious challenge to the established order. For once a woman shows that she can be creatively comic it's not just the content of her work that attracts attention; questions are then asked about women's supposed absence of humour; who says she can't be witty and amusing? Where does such an idea come from – and whose ends does it serve?

---

1. fumerist; I am indebted to Kate Clinton, 1982 for this term; 'Making Light: Another Dimension, Notes on Feminist Humor' in *Trivia: A Journal of Ideas*, Fall, p. 39.

That women are not supposed to have a sense of humour in our society is just another way of saying that it is the male prerogative to tell the jokes. And it takes only one of a number of women's magazines to confirm this. For the woman who wants to be popular is counselled to keep her own wit to herself and to put her energy into laughing at *his* attempts at humour. Even where this is very difficult. As it so often is.

Because many men – and their jokes – are not at all funny. This could be because the jokes themselves are not funny. Or else they are boringly or badly told. Or it could be that they make women the butt of their jokes so that it's no laughing matter for the woman who feels insulted or demeaned. Not that a woman has been allowed to register her negative reaction of course. For while the male joker may be most unfunny, he still has the right to be the joker: and the woman who doesn't laugh is disputing his power, rather than his sense of humour.

So when the man's not funny, and the woman doesn't laugh, it is not he who is in the wrong; she is the one to blame. For she has demonstrated that she has no sense of humour – and no reverence either. The woman who knows her place, knows that it is to laugh on demand, even when the 'joke' is contemptible, cruel or controlling.

Few are the women who have attended mixed sex schools or colleges (or who have been in mixed sex company) who have not been subjected to some of the most unfunny practices, and been required to laugh. At school it was having your plaits put in the inkwell; (today it is having your 'daks' pulled down[2]). And any girl who can't laugh off the male 'teasing', who can't adust to the 'boys will be boys' syndrome, is pulled into line with the further taunt, that she simply can't take a joke. Another woman held up to ridicule because she is judged to have no sense of humour.

According to Anne Beatts who comments on her own socialisation – 'If you were a boy, having a sense of humor meant pouring salt on the head of the girl in front of you so it would look as though she had dandruff. If you were a girl, having a sense of humor meant laughing when someone poured

---

2. 'Dakking' is the practice of many boys in high school; it consists of 'scoring' by pulling down a girl's underpants. For many teenage girls this makes school attendance a nightmare.

salt on your head.' (1975: p.140ff) And she goes on to add, the idea that 'women have no sense of humor' was started by a girl who couldn't put up with the salt being poured on her head, yet again!

And of course, such pressures are not confined to the young. While the (mixed sex) company at an adult dinner party, for example, may be a little more sophisticated, the message that women get is often no less subtle than in the classroom. Learn to put up with the 'jokes', with the teasing, or risk being labelled a prude, a plaintive guest, or a 'party pooper' with no sense of humour. The threat is ever present; when men want to be funny, then women better learn to laugh, or to take the consequences. It's not the women's magazines that suggest that it is just provocation not to laugh at his jokes. (And it is out of the question that a woman should make any jokes of her own: another reason that *fumerists* such as Judy Horacek are breaking new ground.)

And this is why it isn't possible to talk about the art and politics of Judy Horacek's inspirational cartoons, without addressing a very crucial issue – that of the relationship between humour and power. For simply by being funny she breaks the established pattern; and by being funny about authority by mocking some of the practices of patriarchs, she challenges the very nature of power and the subordination of women.[3]

The only humour that women have traditionally been allowed is that of 'getting ' *some* of the jokes told by men. (For the woman who wants approval, it is not advisable to get *all* the jokes; some are considered so outrageous and 'dirty' by the men who tell them, that any woman who 'gets' them, is not demonstrating that she has a sense of humour, but rather is revealing that she is a lascivious and wanton woman.)

In her excellent book, *They Used to Call Me Snow White ... But I Drifted ... Women's Strategic Use of Humor*, (1992) Regina Barreca sums up the dynamics of humour and power; 'A woman who has a good sense of humor is one who laughs (but not too loudly) when a man makes a witticism and

---

3. Margaret Attwood has said that while women are most frightened of being killed, men are most frightened of being mocked. And will react accordingly.

tells a good joke' she quotes.[4] It is a case of *The man provides and the woman receives* (my emphasis; p.7).

The point that is being made here is that women are required to laugh at (some of) the jokes of men, but that they are not supposed to have any comic resources of their own. The fact that men have been the joke tellers is taken as evidence that men have a monopoly on a sense of humour! (What is not so readily or regularly claimed is that men have *monopolised* humour, and used it to reinforce the authority of their own sex.)

Of course the contents of this volume in themselves, expose the falseness and ludicrousness of the assertion that women have no comic sources of their own. But before taking up the issue of women's autonomous (and abundant) source of wit and wisdom, there is more to be said about women's non-participation in the customary joke-making of society.

There can be no doubt that men have declared the traditional forms of humour to be a boys' game and have determined to keep women out. But neither can there be any doubt that most women have not been impressed by the game, and have decided that they do not want to play.

This is partly because it has been common practice for the joke teller, the humourist, to 'seize the floor', to monopolise attention, claim space, and insist on his own view of the world and his own right to speak; and none of these characteristics sits comfortably with women's customary conversation codes. (While little research has been undertaken on women and humour – in part no doubt because it would be difficult to get research money to investigate something which is not supposed to exist – what evidence there is seems to indicate that women are more likely to find a situation funny, that they are more likely to collaborate in a funny story, that they are more likely to question the order of the world rather than exploit stereotypes, or make fun of individual human beings – as is the case with most 'joke' telling.)

---

4. Regina Barreca is actually quoting from the psychologist Rose Laub Coser 'Laughter Among Colleagues', *Psychiatry* 23 (February 1960) 81–95.

'Much male humour is aggressive and attempts to be controlling' (1992: p. 180) states Regina Barreca outlining some of the reasons that women have elected to stay out of the traditional funny forum. And this is not all. Much of male humour also assumes a victim – the ethnic joke, the stereotype joke of the mother-in-law etc. – and this is where female and male humour can part company.[5]

'Women do not often laugh at the genuine misfortunes of others – women are, according to the psychoanalyst Natalie Becker, less likely than men to laugh at a situation where someone is hurt or embarrassed. Women are more likely to attempt to console than laugh at anyone who can be considered a victim. This is perhaps one of the reasons that certain forms of slapstick comedy appeal far less to women than to men: when the Three Stooges poke one another in the eye, women tend to wince or sigh, more than laugh' (Regina Barreca, 1992: p.12).

In her article 'Female Wits' Emily Toth (1981) has referred to this practice among women as the operation of 'the humane humor rule'. Basically it means that women do not seek to make fun of 'handicaps' that people cannot change. While women may mock, expose, satirise and even make jokes that reflect their own perspective, rarely are there any *scapegoats* in women's humorous anecdotes and exchanges. 'Rather,' says Emily Toth, 'women humorists attack – or subvert – the deliberate choices people make; hypocrisies, affectations, mindless following of social expectations'. And it is this which leads Regina Barreca to name one of the fundamental differences between women's humour, and that of men; '*women's comedy takes as its material the powerful, rather than the pitiful*' (my emphasis; p.13).

It isn't that women have no sense of humour; it is that *for very good reasons*, they don't usually have the same sense of humour as men. And this isn't just in relation to the victim, the scapegoat, the butt of the joke. Women also use humour for different ends; it is one of the strategies for promoting common understandings among women – and for promoting change.

---

5. There are, of course, exceptions amongst men: those who've read widely on feminism (or have lived with a feminist); or those who come from a group suffering some sort of discrimination (men with disabilities, Blacks, gays, etc.); though membership of these groups is no guarantee.

While men, of course, have had digs at the conventions of the world, and have poked fun at institutions and establishments, they lack 'the truly anarchic edge that characterizes feminine humor' Regina Barreca claims. The hallmark of women's humour 'is that it calls into question the largest issues, (it) questions the way the world is put together . . . (it) has a particular interest in challenging the most formidable structures because they keep women from positions of power' (p.179). Women's humour is part of the revolution.

And this is where the art and politics of the woman humorist meet; it is where the work of Judy Horacek makes such a marvellous contribution. For she takes subjects that are 'beyond a joke' as the source of her cartoon humour. She gives voice to women's view and vision in a succinct and satiric way; and as the American poet Marianne Moore has said – 'Humor saves a few steps; it saves years'. *Life on the Edge* gets us there much more quickly.

The cartoon form imposes its own demands. It must sum up, change the perspective, indicate identity and values. And a feminist cartoon usually challenges authority, and helps us to laugh at what we have been taught to revere. And this in itself is boundary breaking and revolutionary. For, as Regina Barreca says, 'when women laugh together, we underscore the ways in which our experiences of the world connect us rather than divide us' (p.186). Which is why women cannot look at *Life on the Edge* and not be moved; preferably away from the oppressive elements of society and to a more satisfactory environment!!

All the literature that attempts to define humour suggests that it lies in the incongruity between what is known, and what might be. And if this is so, such definitions could have been written with the work of Judy Horacek in mind. For she directs her caustic eye to the known constraints placed upon women and plays with the possibilities, so that she 'switches things round' and gives women's world a new focus. And if the pomp and power of men is eroded in the process, the result can be sobering – and entertaining.

Understandably men do not like their precious precepts and practices subjected to fumerist scrutiny and made fun of; but what women can find amusing is how few men actually 'get' the meanings of women's jokes and cartoons. (And how radical would it be to start to suggest that it is men who have no sense of humour?) And if and when they do appreciate the irreverence and subversion of such talented women as Judy Horacek, it is worth remembering the words of the nineteenth-century American essayist Agnes Reppelier – that 'only false gods are laughed off their earthly pedestals' (see Regina Barreca, p.179).

In her book, *Stitches: a patchwork of feminist humor and satire* (1991) Gloria Kaufman states that feminist humour is hopeful rather than resigned; that it is celebratory rather than bitter. She shows how it is brazenly political in that it is used to help people break out of the place in which they have been confined. Feminist humour is a courageous and clever form of resistance; in concentrating on the politics it subverts the myth of the powerlessness of women. It offers hope; it dispels fear.

And Judy Horacek's creative cartoons meet all these criteria.

Not only does she defy the adage that women have no sense of humour – *and* challenge the conventional wisdom that women also lack political astuteness (and there's no need to look far to find where such fancies come from) – Judy Horacek also empowers us to think and act in positive ways that enhance our future and which frame a more just society. To do this in a way that draws us to levity and laughter and liberation, is a remarkable achievement.

REFERENCES

Barreca, Regina, 1992, *They Used to Call Me Snow White … But I Drifted: Women's Strategic Use of Humor*, Penguin/Viking, New York.

Beatts, Anne, 1975, 'Can a Woman Get a Laugh and a Man Too?' *Mademoiselle*, November, 1400ff.

Clinton, Kate, 1982, 'Making Light: Another Dimension, Notes on Feminist Humor', *Trivia: A Journal of Ideas*, Fall, p. 39.

Kaufman, Gloria (ed.) 1990, *Stitches: a patchwork of feminist humor and satire*, Indiana University Press, Indiana & Bloomington.

Toth, Emily, 1981, 'Female Wits', *Massachusetts Review 22*, no. 4, (Winter), pp. 783–793.

Dale Spender, August 1992

These cartoons have been previously published in the following publications:

The Age, Accent, 20 Oct 1989, Page 68; 27 Dec 1989, Page 71; Aidex campaign, 1991, Page 22; Art Monthly, 49, May 1992, Page 76a; ARU Gazette, March 1991, Page 23b; March 1992, Page 30; As I was saying: The Wit & Wisdom of Australian Women, compiled by Margaret Geddes, Five Mile Press, Balwyn, 1990, Page 16a & b; Page 74b; Australia Council Magazine, Page 34a; Australian Feminist Book Fortnight logo, 1989, Page v; Australian Left Review, No, 122, Aug 1990, Page 67; No. 127, March 1991, Page 84; No. 128, May 1991, Page 25; No. 129, June 1991, Page 41; No. 131, Aug 1991, Page 37; No. 133, Oct 1991, Page 72b; No. 134, November 1991, Page 24; No. 136, Feb 1992, Page 53; No. 136, Feb 1992, Page 85; No. 137, March 1992, Page 81; No. 138, April 1992, Page 36b; No. 140, June 1992, Page 74a; No. 141, July 1992, Page 23a; Australian Society, Feb 1989, Page 39a; August 1989, Page 5a; October 1989, Page 21; December 1989/January 1990, Page 9a; Page 58a & b; April 1990, Page 48a; March 1991, Page 54a; May 1991, Page 6; June 1991, Page 7a; July 1991, Page 42a; August 1991, Page 73; Oct 1991, Page 55a; November 1991, Page 42b; December 1991, Page 10; Australian Teacher, May 1990, Page 52; Australian Women's Studies Association logo, 1990, Title page; Beyond a Joke, ed. Kaz Cooke, McPhee Gribble/Penguin, 1988, Page 13a; Centrefold, Victorian Writers Centre Bulletin, Page 76b; Christmas cards, 1989, Page 79; 1990, Page 12b; Page 86; Curbin' the Urban community arts project, Princes Hill School Park Centre, North Carlton, 1990, Page 2; Page 8; Page 11a & b; Page 40; Page 49b; Page 61a & b; Page 62a & b; Page 78b; Page 80a & b; Directory of Self Help Groups, 5th ed., Collective of Self Help Groups, Melbourne 1989, Page 34b; Page 72a; Drawing Away No. 6, Newtown, 1991, Page 17; Girls Own Annual, Deakin Women's Studies Summer Institute, 1989, Page 5b; Greeting cards, 1992, Page 63; Page 69; A Handle on Work, compiled by Renate Tratter, Council of Adult Education, Page 7b; Health Issues, No. 15, September 1988, Page 20a; No. 22, March 1990, Page 9b; No. 23, June 1990, Page 49a; Who controls where the health dollar goes, Health Issues Centre, 1992, Page 46; Page 47a; Law Handbook, 1989, Fitzroy Legal Service, Page 12a; Page 56b; Legal Service Bulletin, Vol. 14, No. 2, April 1989, Page 26b; Vol. 14, No. 3, June 1989, Page 39b; Vol. 15, No. 1, February 1990, Page 27; Vol. 15, No. 3, June 1990, Page 32; Vol. 16, No. 1, Feb 1991, Page 31; Vol. 16, No. 3, June 1991, Page 29; Meanjin, No. 1, 1992 Autumn, Page 3; Page 64; Page 65; Page 77; No. 2, 1992 Winter, Page 13b; Modern Times, No. 2, April 1992, Page 4; May 1992, Page 35; July 1992, Page 51; Page 83; September 1992, Page 70; Perseverance Poets Collection, 1991–92, Perseverance Poets Collective, Melbourne 1992, Page 47b; Postcards, 1992, Page 1; Page 33; Page 59; Page 78a; Reclaim the Night, booklet distributed at march, 1988, Page 14a & b; Page 50a & b; Reclaim the Night poster, 1988, Page 15; Socialist Objective, Vol. 10, No. 1, May/June 1990, Page 28; Users Guide 1990, Fitzroy Legal Service, Page 55b; Page 56a; VCE Music booklet, Occupational Health and Safety Commission, 1991, Page 36a.

First publication cited only.

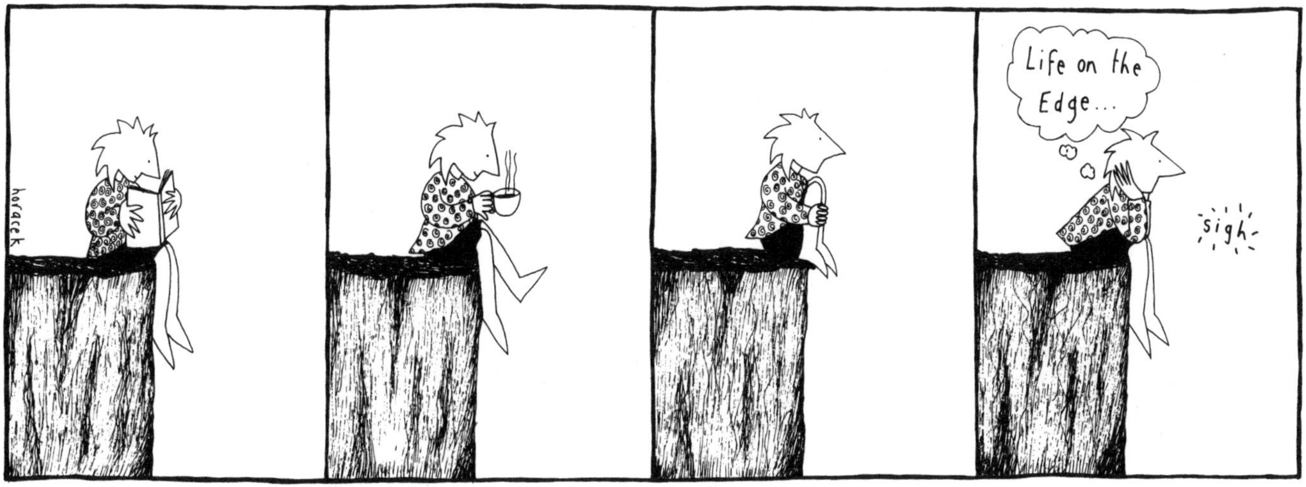
horacek
Life on the Edge...
sigh

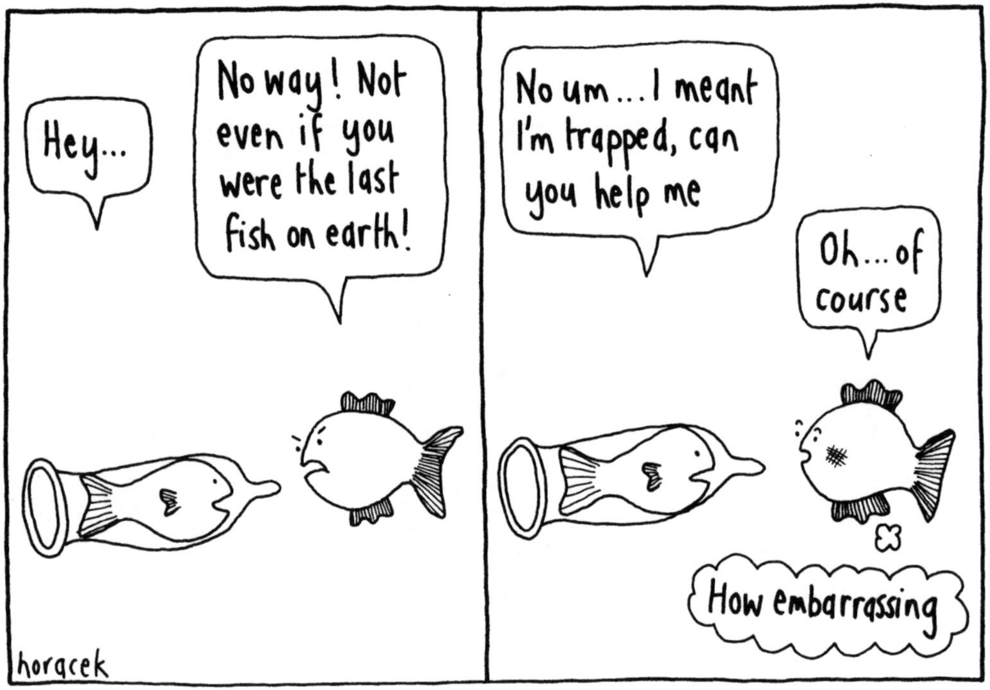
Hey...
No way! Not even if you were the last fish on earth!
No um... I meant I'm trapped, can you help me
Oh... of course
How embarrassing
horacek

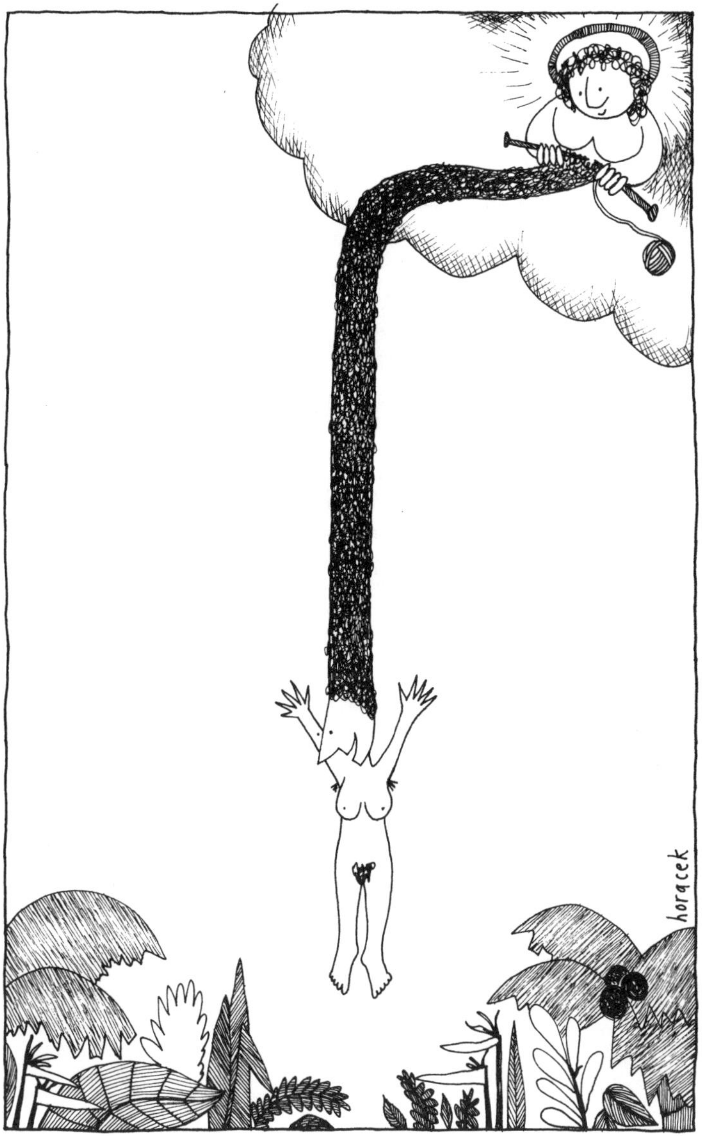
horacek

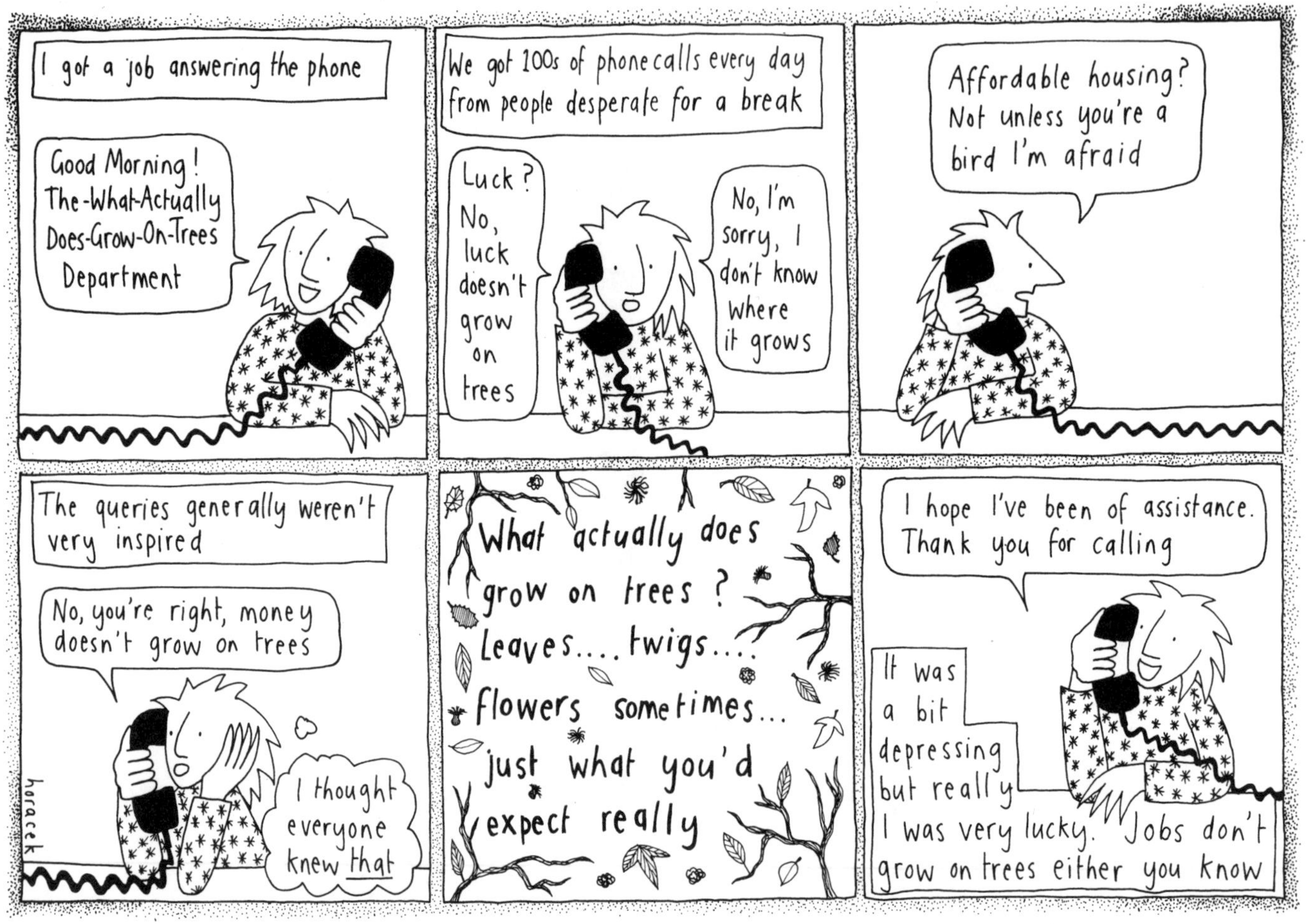
I got a job answering the phone
Good Morning! The-What-Actually Does-Grow-On-Trees Department
We got 100s of phone calls every day from people desperate for a break
Luck? No, luck doesn't grow on trees
No, I'm sorry, I don't know where it grows
Affordable housing? Not unless you're a bird I'm afraid
The queries generally weren't very inspired
No, you're right, money doesn't grow on trees
I thought everyone knew that
horacek
What actually does grow on trees? Leaves.... twigs.... flowers sometimes... just what you'd expect really
I hope I've been of assistance. Thank you for calling
It was a bit depressing but really I was very lucky. Jobs don't grow on trees either you know

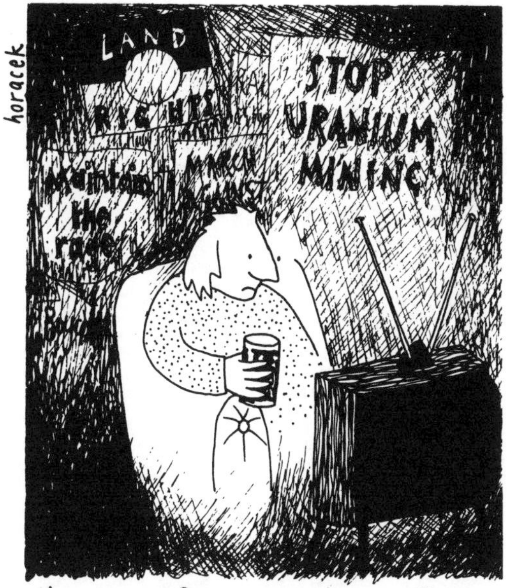
horacek
LAND
STOP URANIUM MINING

He never fully recovered from the discovery that ASIO didn't have a file on him

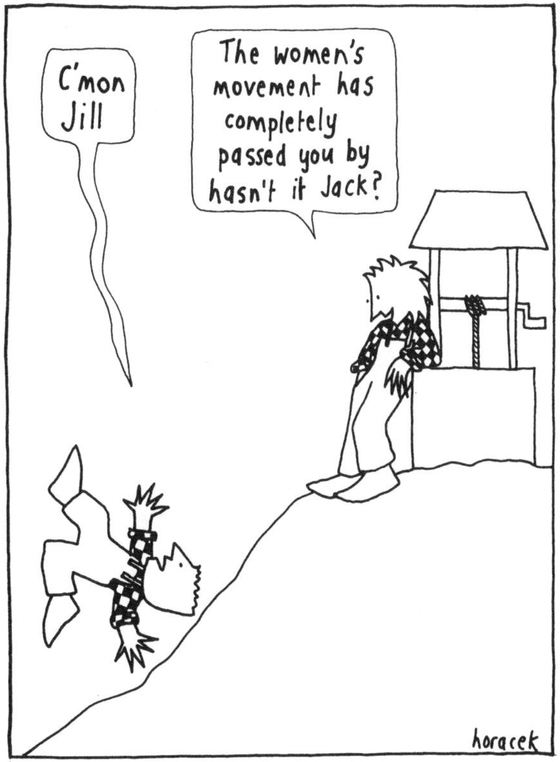
C'mon Jill
The women's movement has completely passed you by hasn't it Jack?
horacek

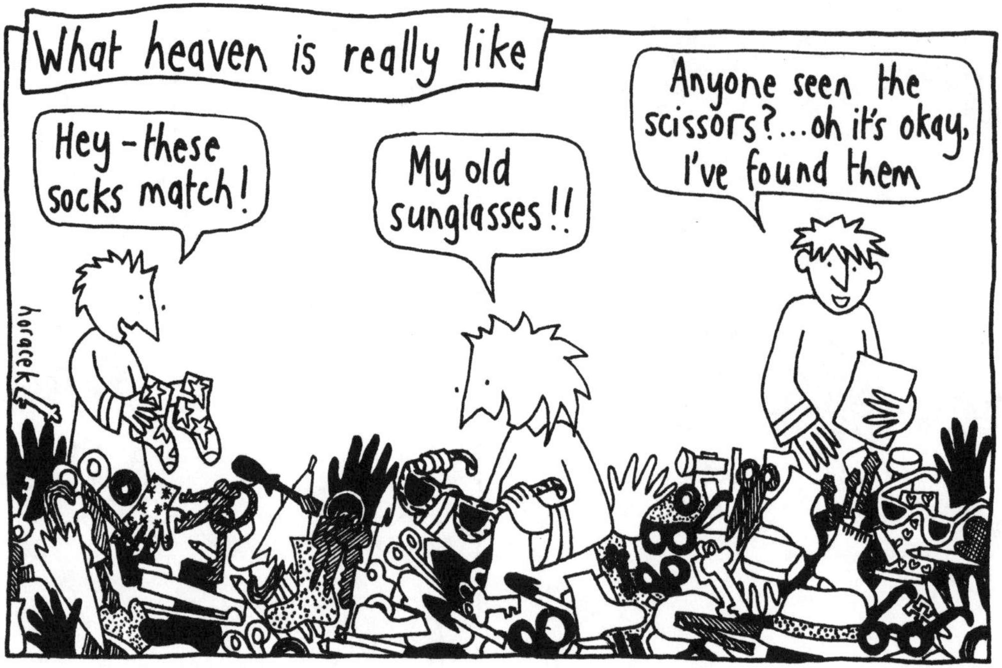
What heaven is really like
Hey - these socks match!
My old sunglasses!!
Anyone seen the scissors?... oh it's okay, I've found them
horacek

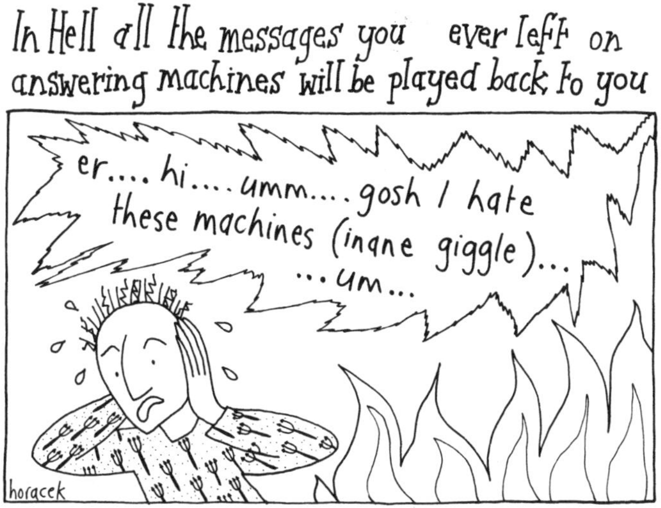
In Hell all the messages you ever left on answering machines will be played back to you
er.... hi.... umm.... gosh I hate these machines (inane giggle)... ...um...
horacek

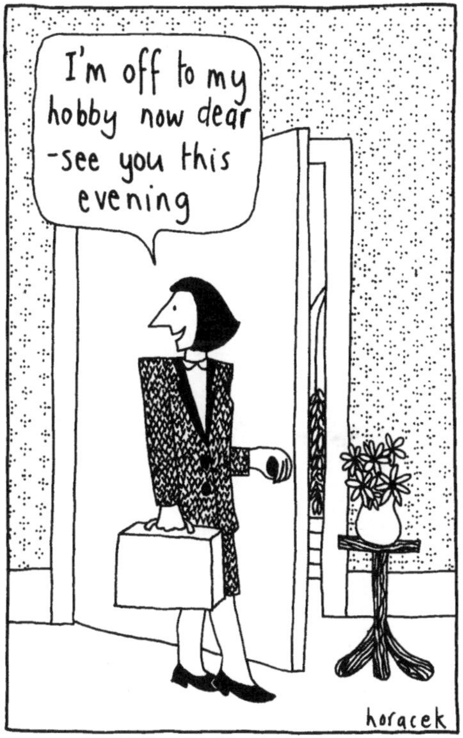
I'm off to my hobby now dear -see you this evening
horacek

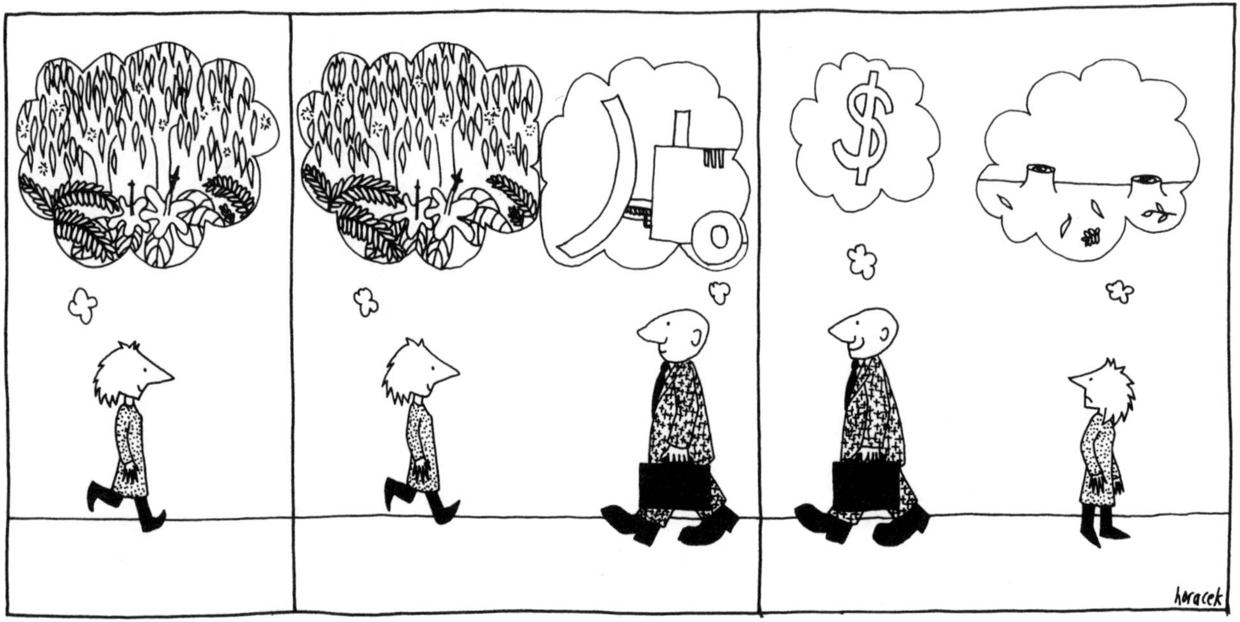
$
horacek

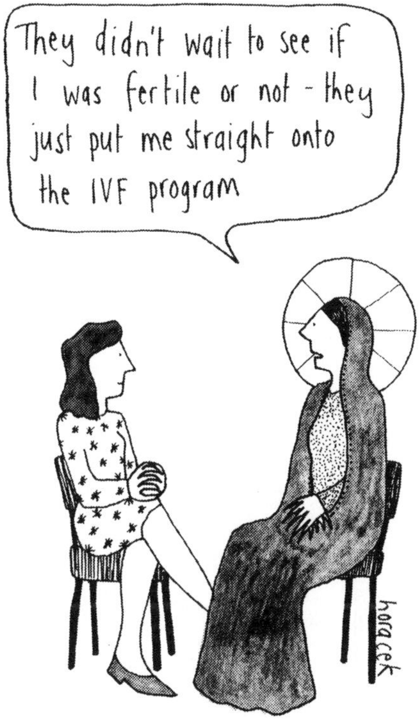
They didn't wait to see if I was fertile or not - they just put me straight onto the IVF program
horacek

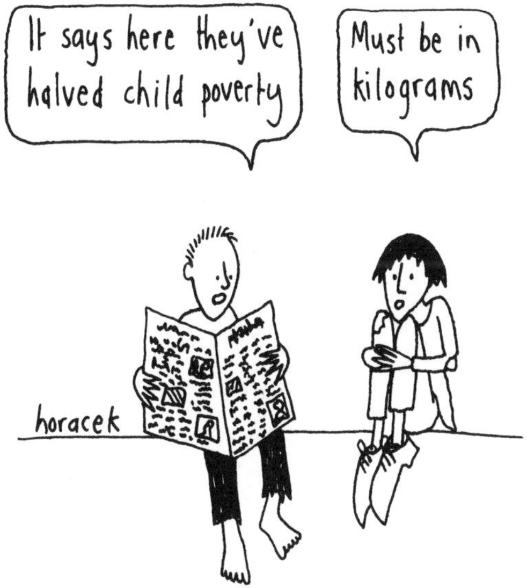
It says here they've halved child poverty
Must be in kilograms
horacek

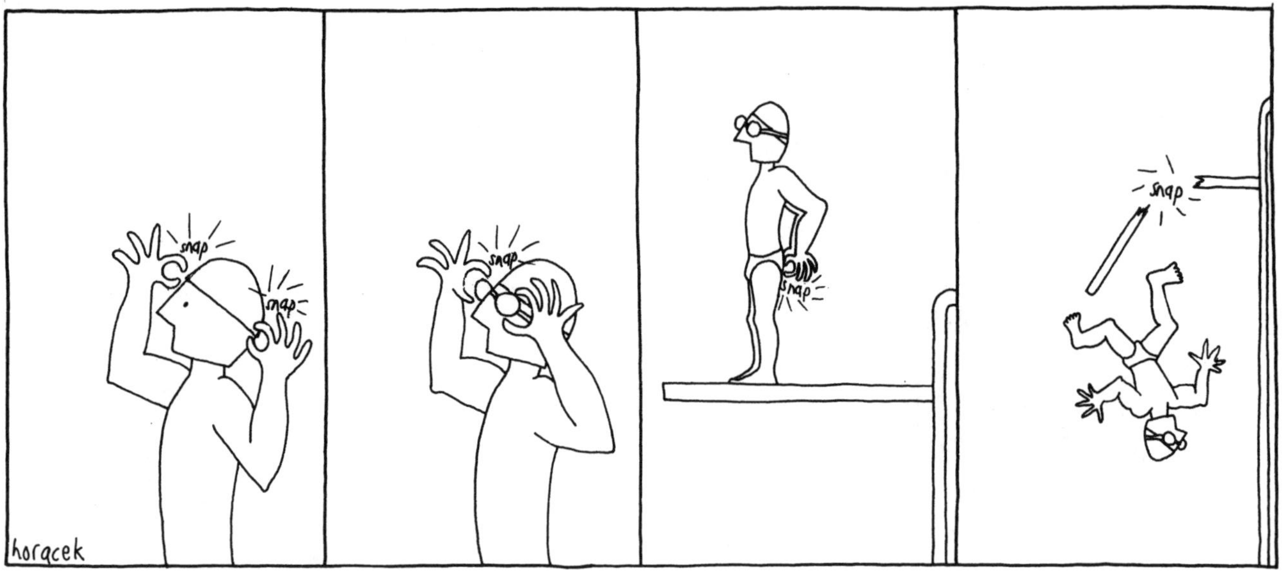
snap
snap
snap
snap
snap
snap
horacek

After the oil slick ...
horacek

horacek

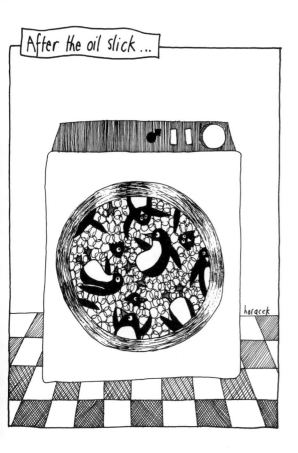

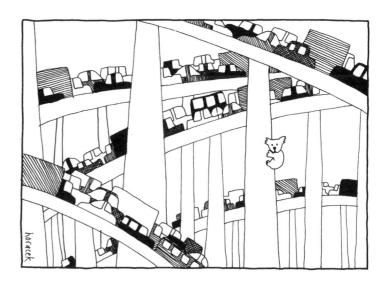

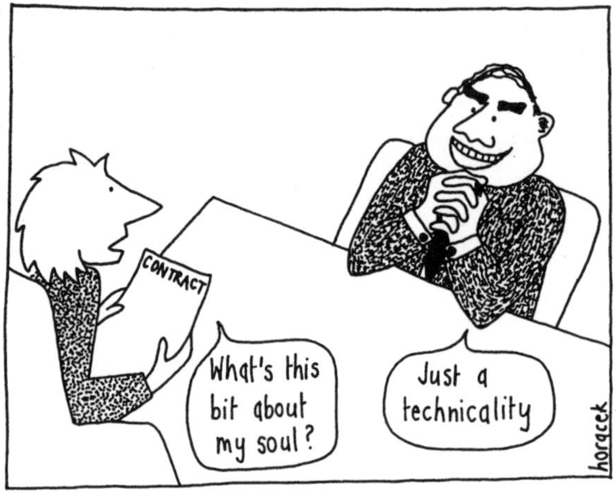
CONTRACT
What's this bit about my soul?
Just a technicality
horacek

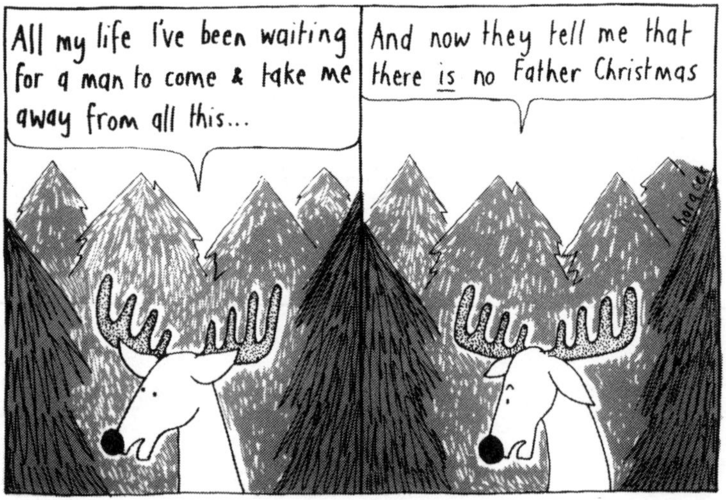
All my life I've been waiting for a man to come & take me away from all this...
And now they tell me that there is no Father Christmas
horacek

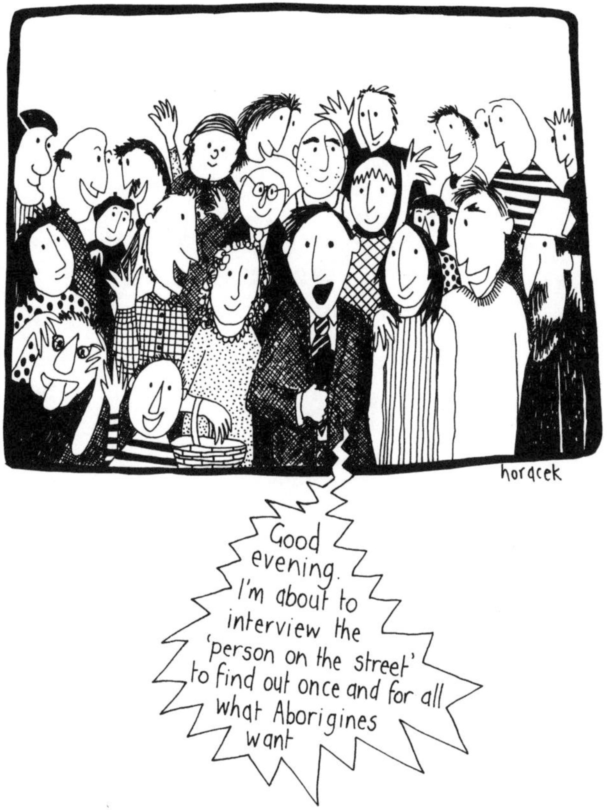
horacek
Good evening. I'm about to interview the 'person on the street' to find out once and for all what Aborigines want

How T-shirts can save your life

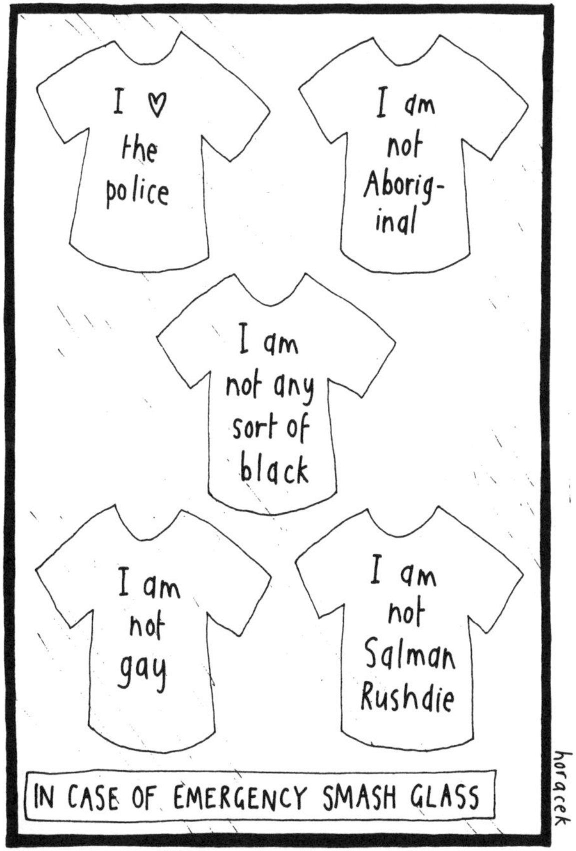
I ♡ the police
I am not Aboriginal
I am not any sort of black
I am not gay
I am not Salman Rushdie
IN CASE OF EMERGENCY SMASH GLASS
horacek

Coming Soon: Tattoos for Health & Safety

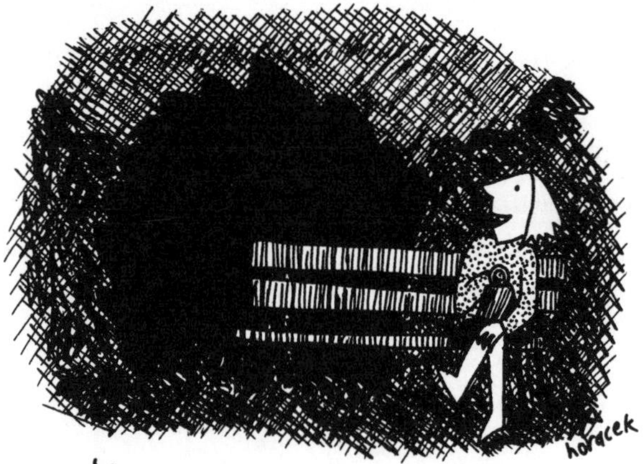
horacek

'Aren't you scared being alone?' said a sleazy voice from the bushes. 'Being alone is what I want' she replied, reaching into her handbag for her new improved vaporising gun.

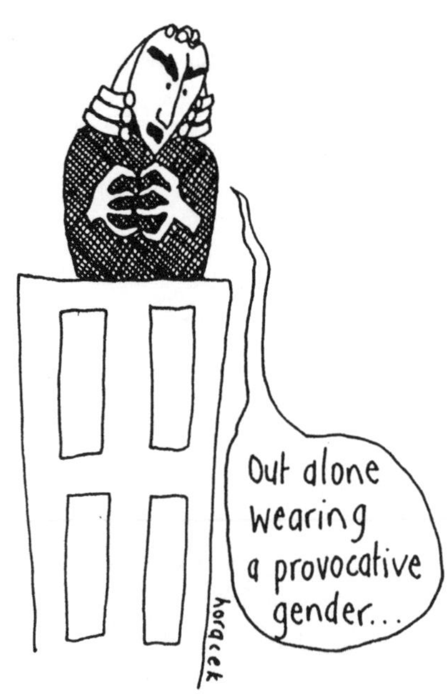
Out alone wearing a provocative gender...
horacek

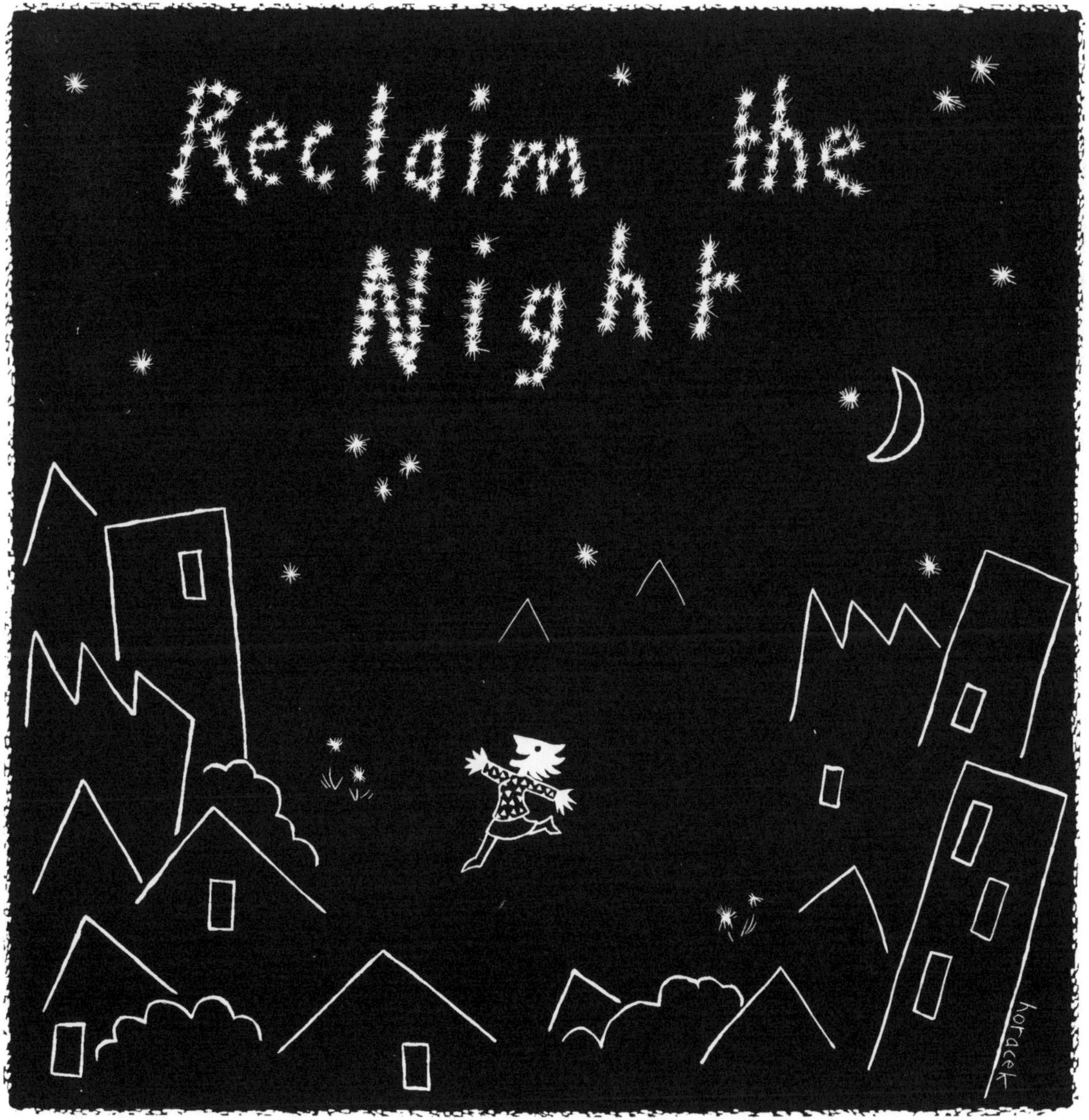
Reclaim the Night
horacek

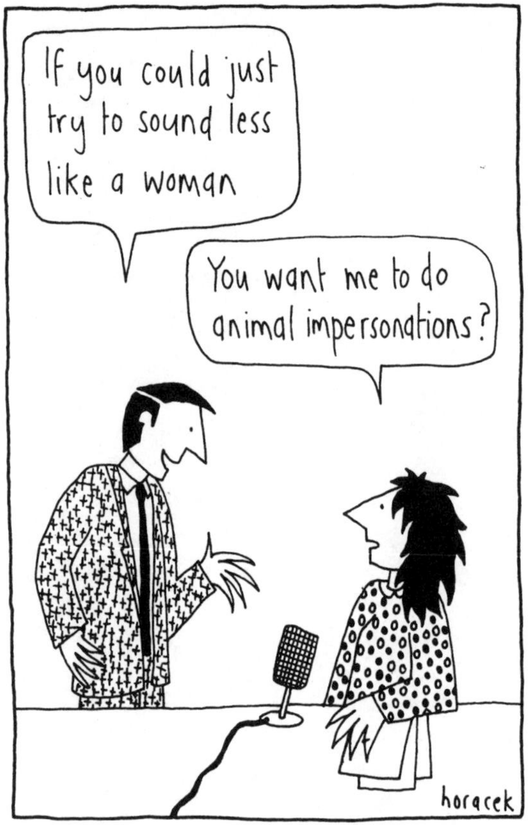
If you could just try to sound less like a woman
You want me to do animal impersonations?
horacek

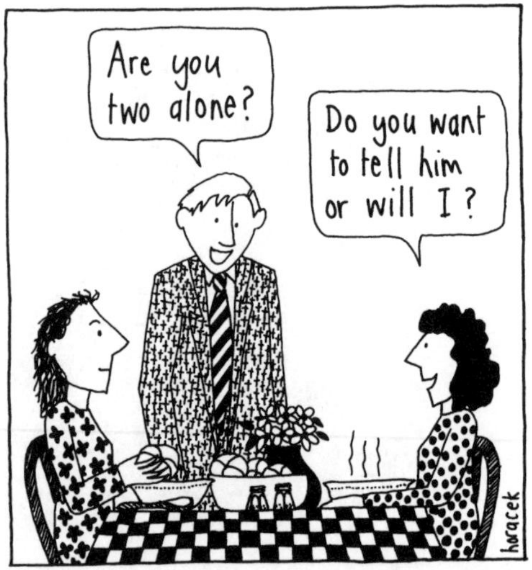
Are you two alone?
Do you want to tell him or will I?
horacek

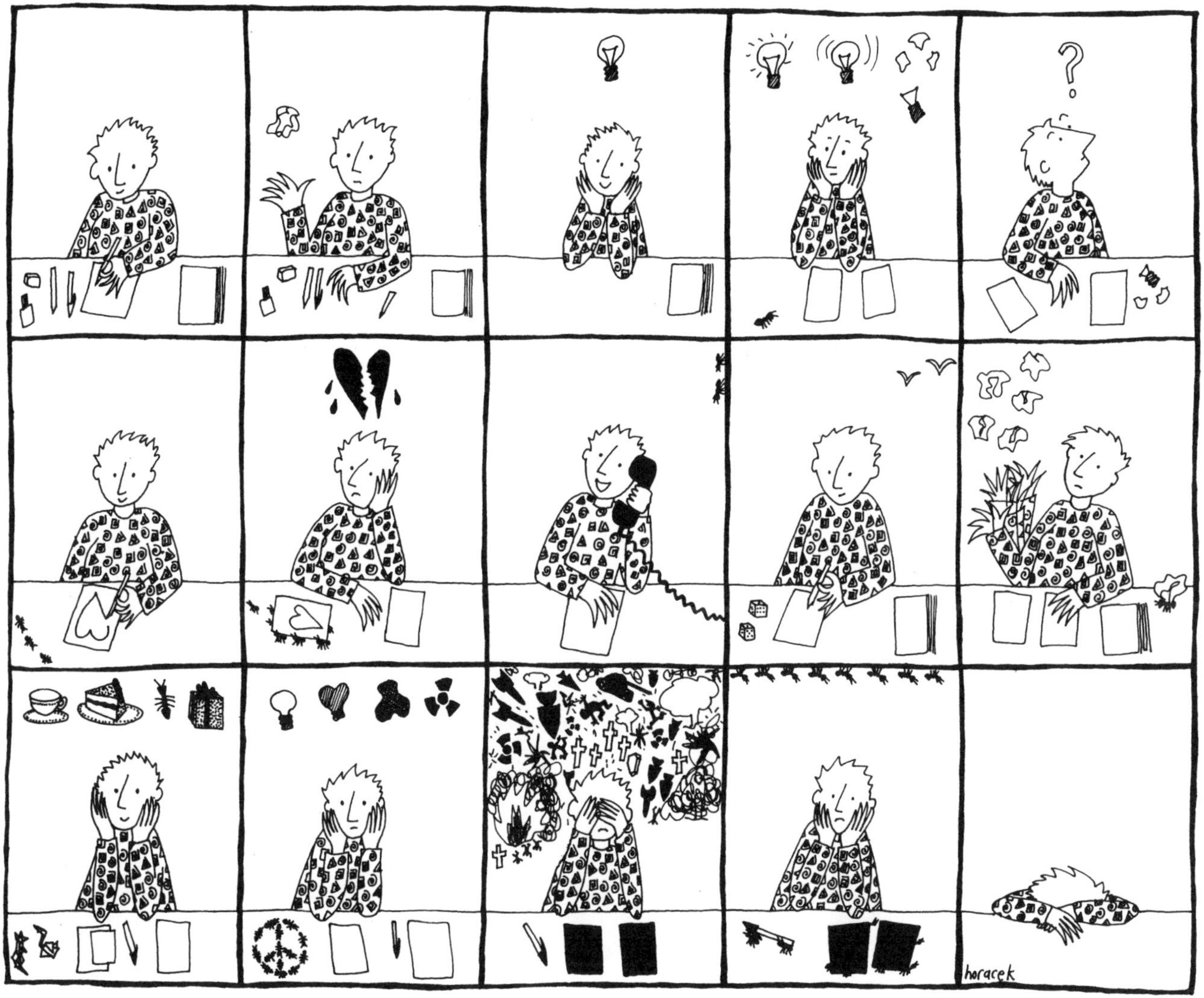
horacek

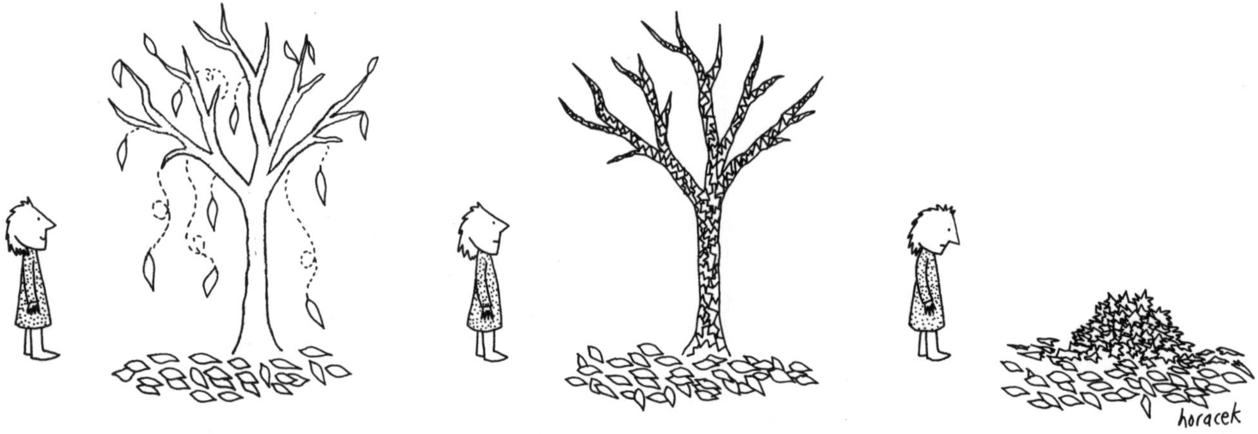
horacek

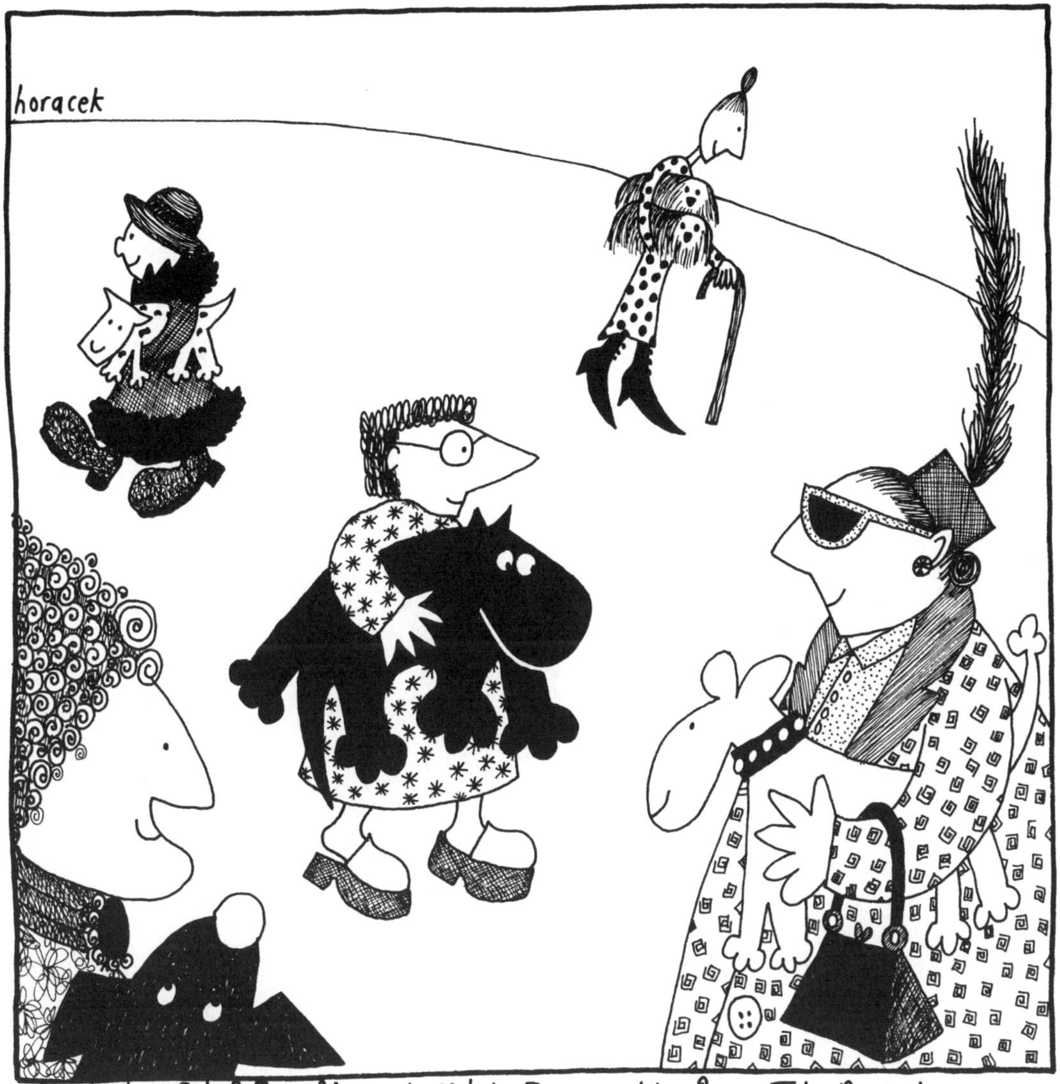
horacek

Little Old Ladies With Dogs Under Their Arms

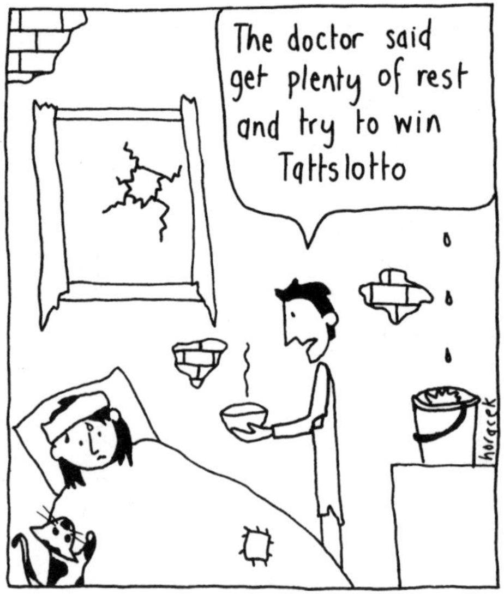
The doctor said get plenty of rest and try to win Tattslotto
horacek

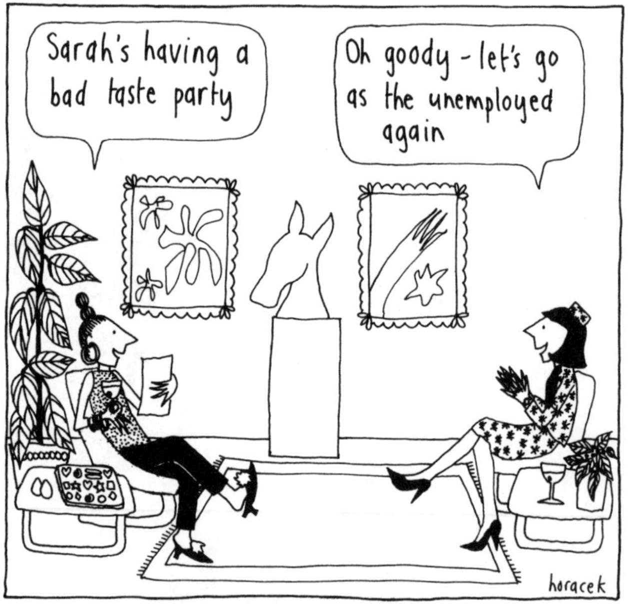
Sarah's having a bad taste party
Oh goody - let's go as the unemployed again
horacek

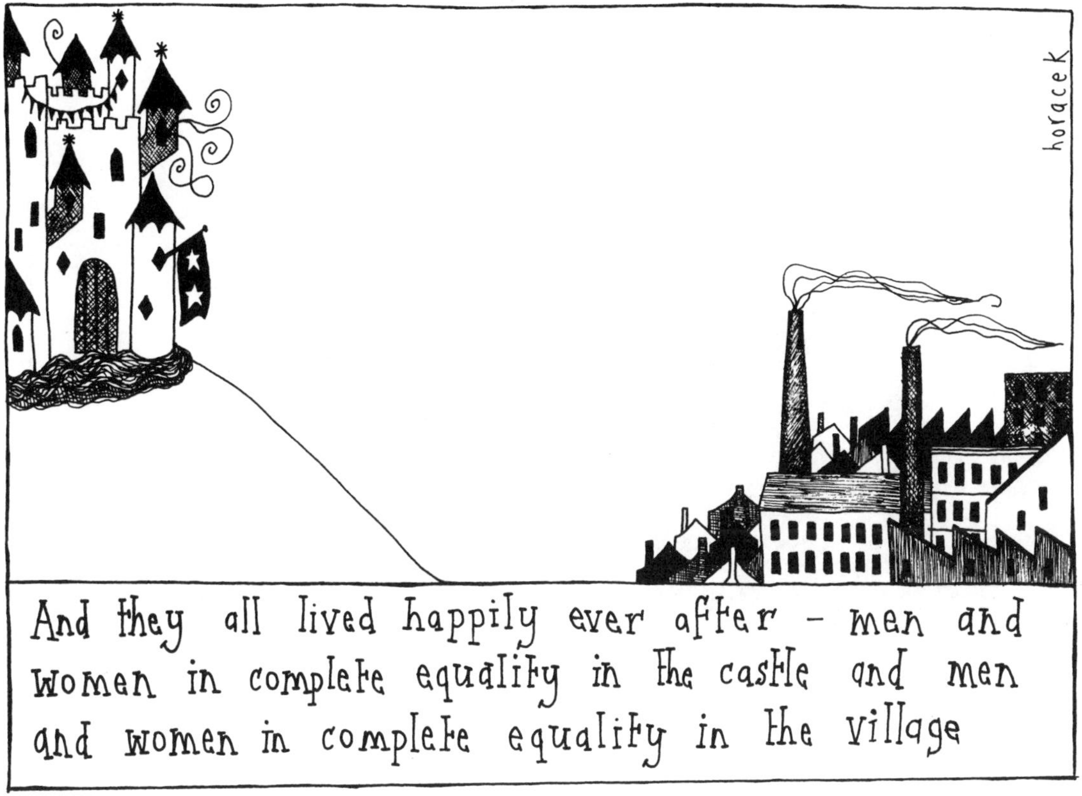
horacek
And they all lived happily ever after - men and women in complete equality in the castle and men and women in complete equality in the village

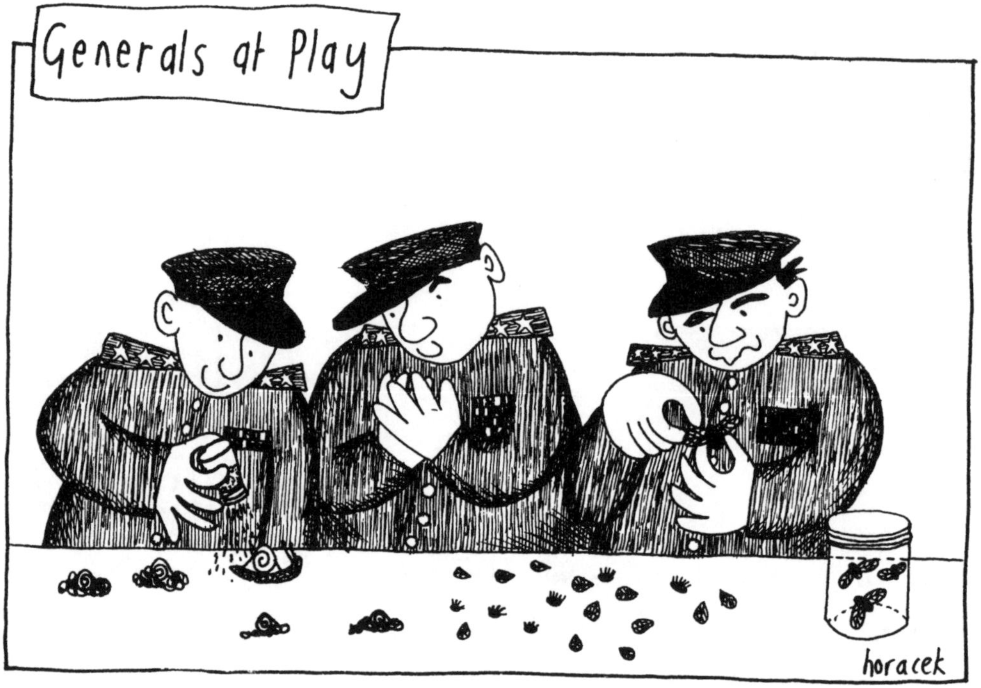
Generals at Play
horacek

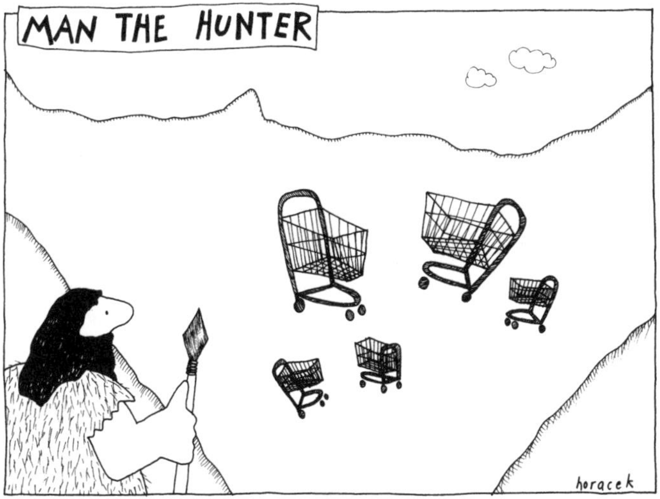
MAN THE HUNTER
horacek

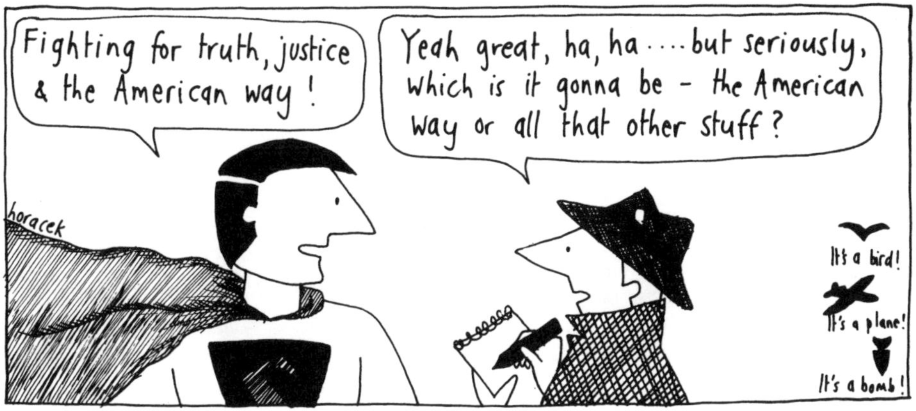
Fighting for truth, justice & the American way !
Yeah great, ha, ha .... but seriously, which is it gonna be - the American way or all that other stuff ?
horacek
It's a bird!
It's a plane!
It's a bomb!

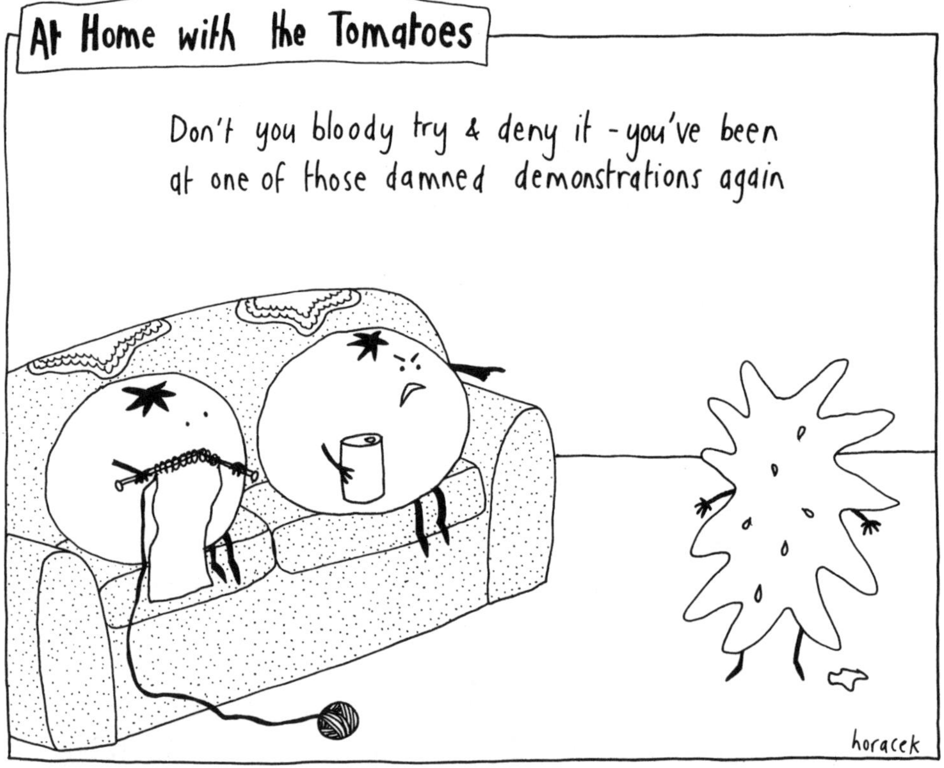
At Home with the Tomatoes
Don't you bloody try & deny it - you've been at one of those damned demonstrations again
horacek

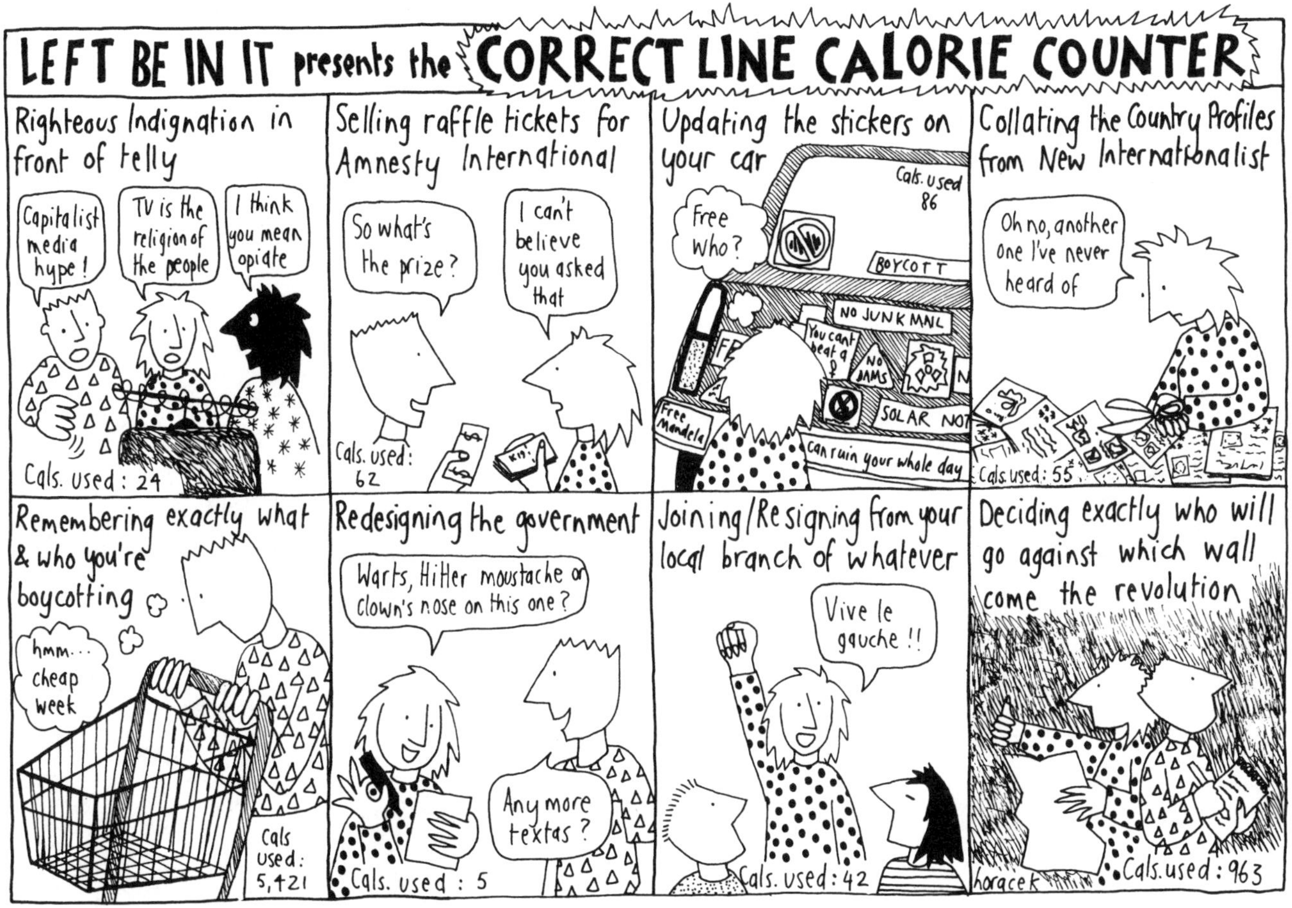
LEFT BE IN IT presents the CORRECT LINE CALORIE COUNTER
Righteous Indignation in front of telly
Capitalist media hype!
TV is the religion of the people
I think you mean opiate
Cals. used: 24
Selling raffle tickets for Amnesty International
So what's the prize?
I can't believe you asked that
Cals. used: 62
Updating the stickers on your car
Free who?
Cals. used 86
BOYCOTT
NO JUNK MAIL
You can't beat a ♀
NO DAMS
SOLAR NOT
Free Mandela
can ruin your whole day
Collating the Country Profiles from New Internationalist
Oh no, another one I've never heard of
Cals. used: 55
Remembering exactly what & who you're boycotting
hmm... cheap week
Cals used: 5,421
Redesigning the government
Warts, Hitler moustache or clown's nose on this one?
Any more textas?
Cals. used: 5
Joining/Resigning from your local branch of whatever
Vive le gauche!!
Cals. used: 42
Deciding exactly who will go against which wall come the revolution
Cals. used: 963
horacek

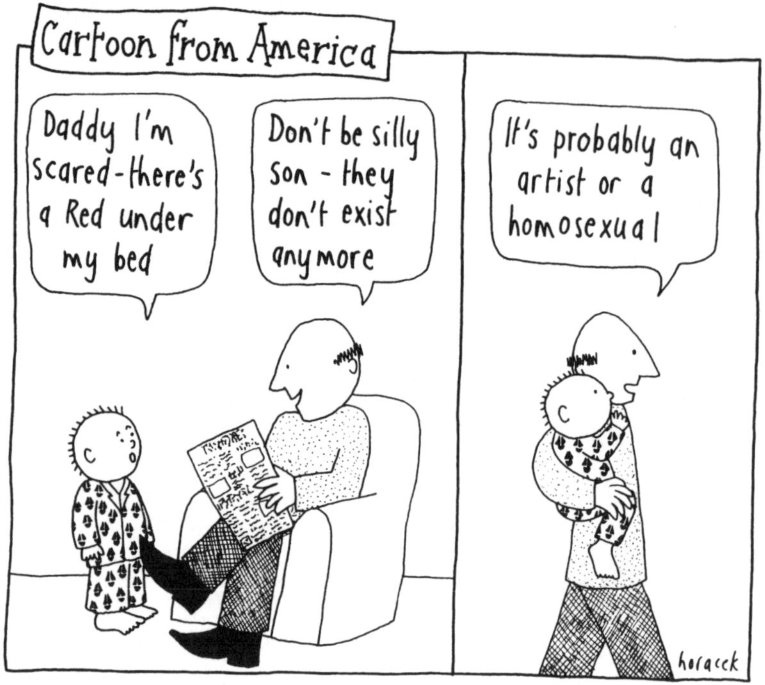
Cartoon from America
Daddy I'm scared - there's a Red under my bed
Don't be silly son - they don't exist anymore
It's probably an artist or a homosexual
horacek

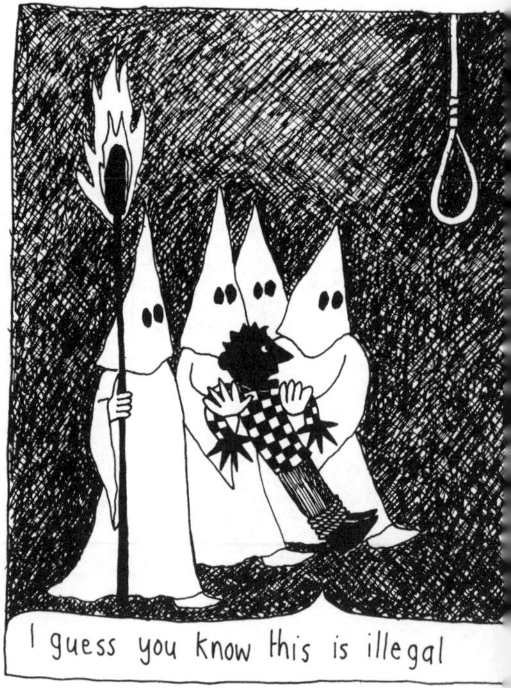
I guess you know this is illegal

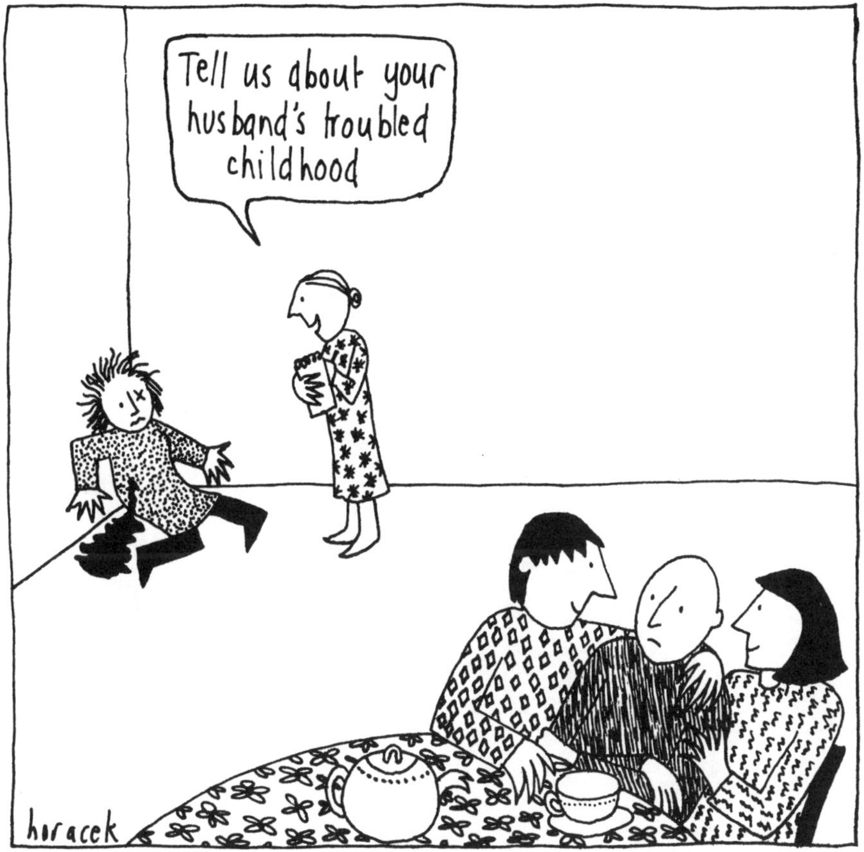
Tell us about your husband's troubled childhood
horacek

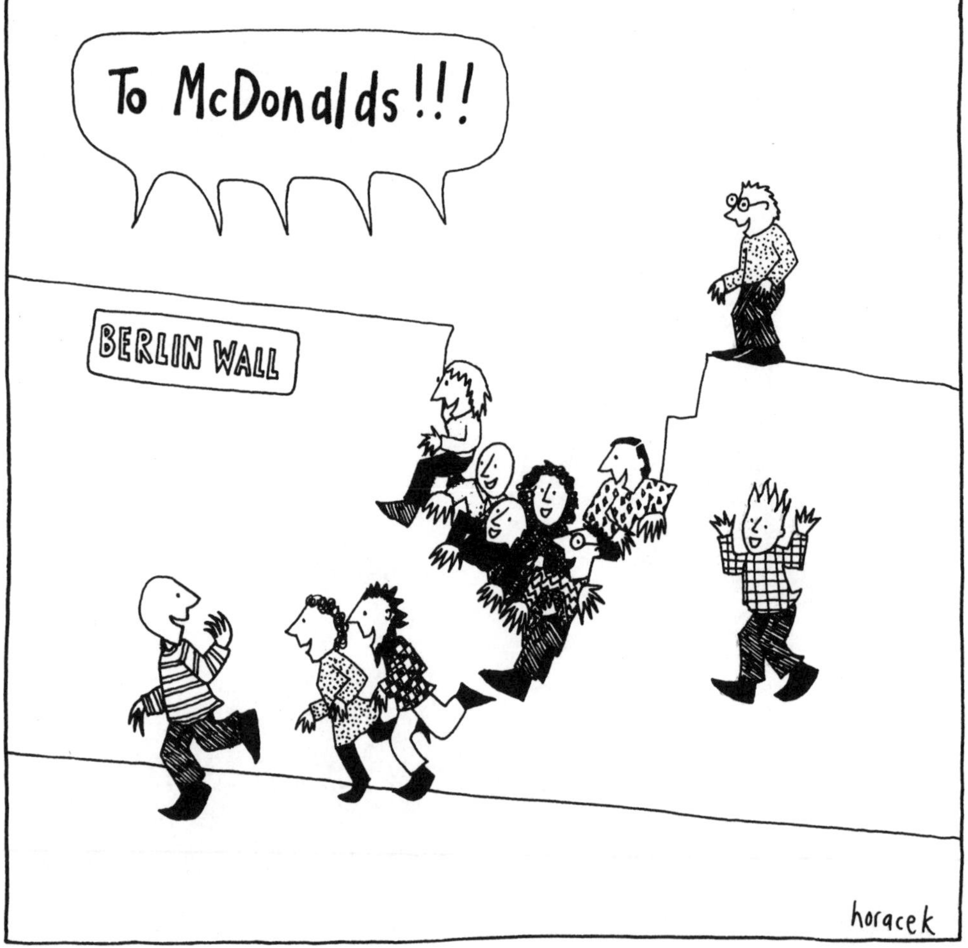
To McDonalds!!!
BERLIN WALL
horacek

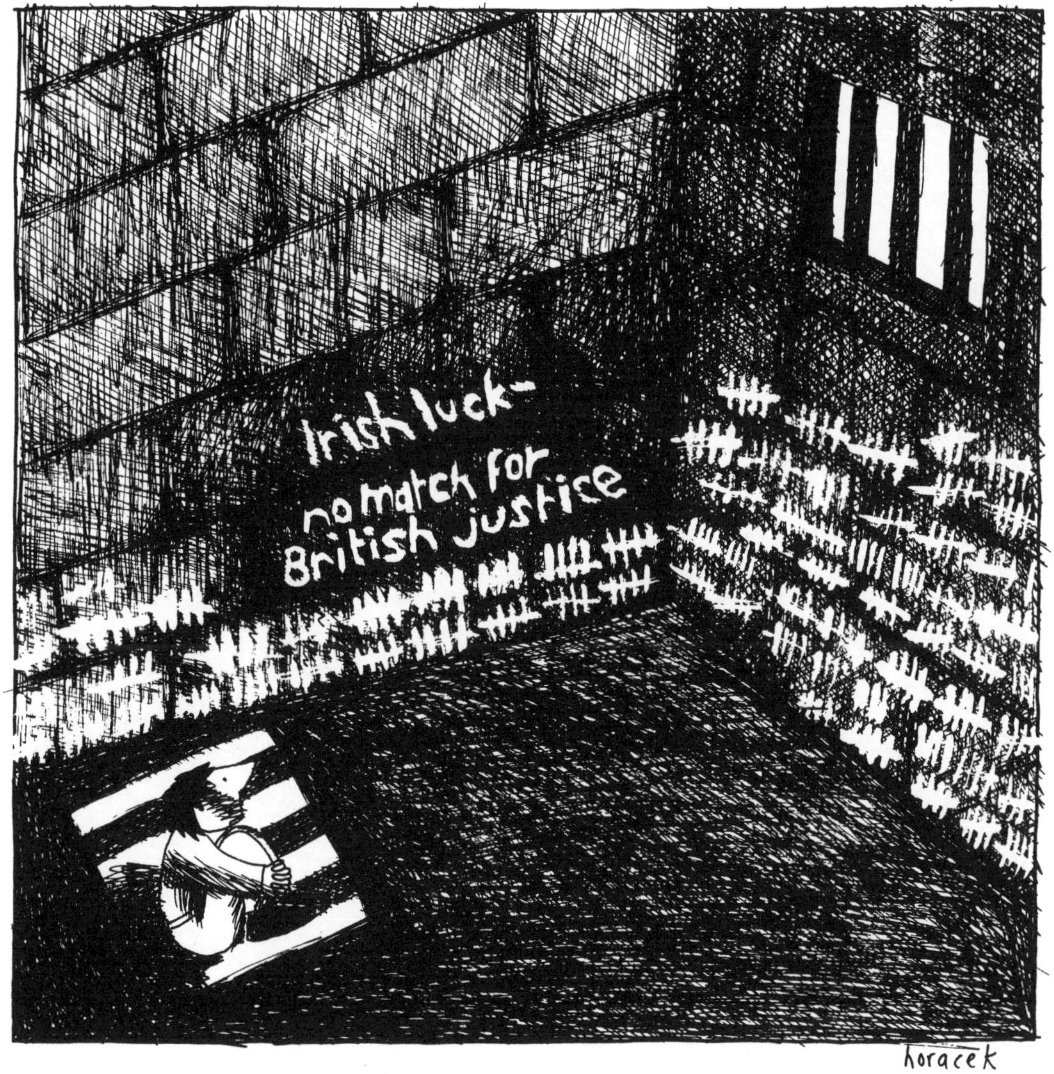
Irish luck-
no match for
British justice
horacek

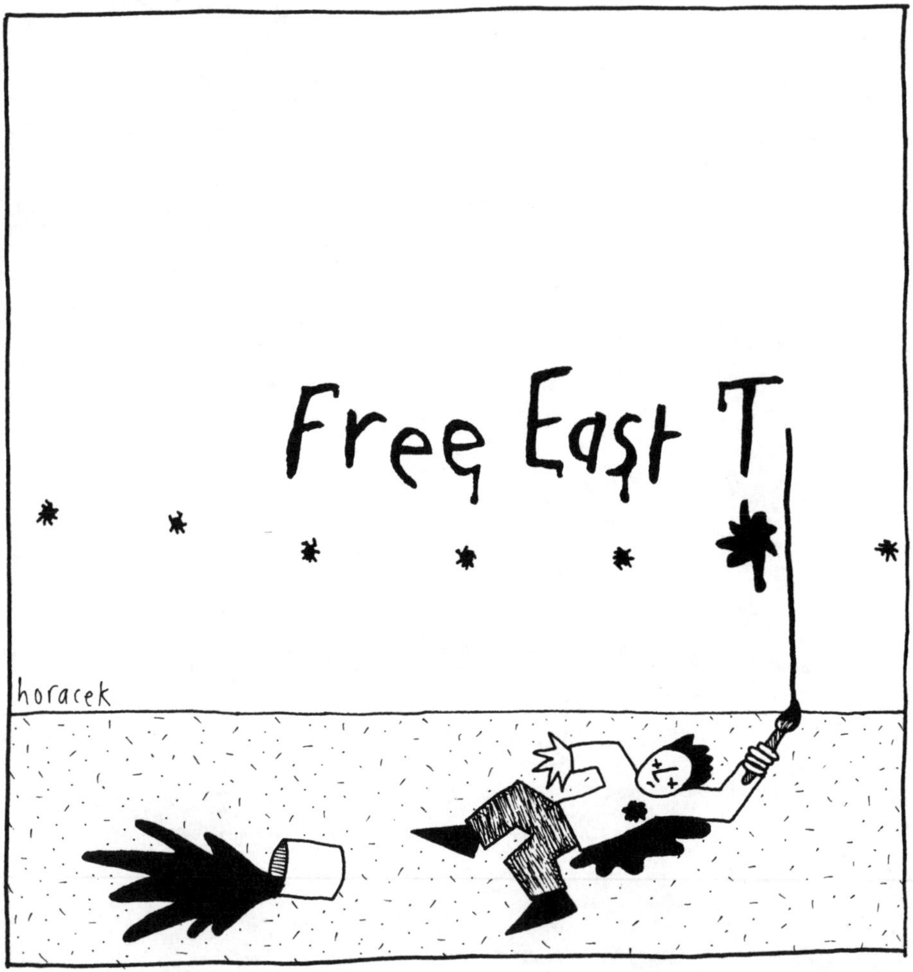
Free East T
horacek

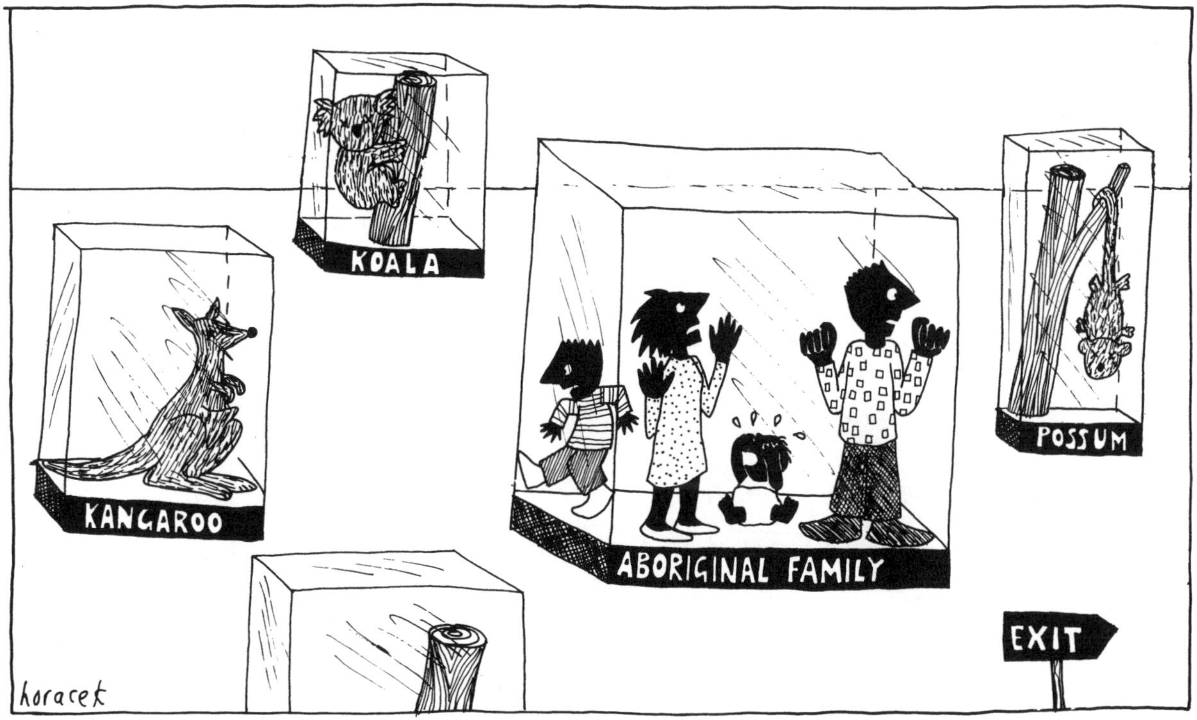
KOALA
KANGAROO
ABORIGINAL FAMILY
POSSUM
EXIT
horacek

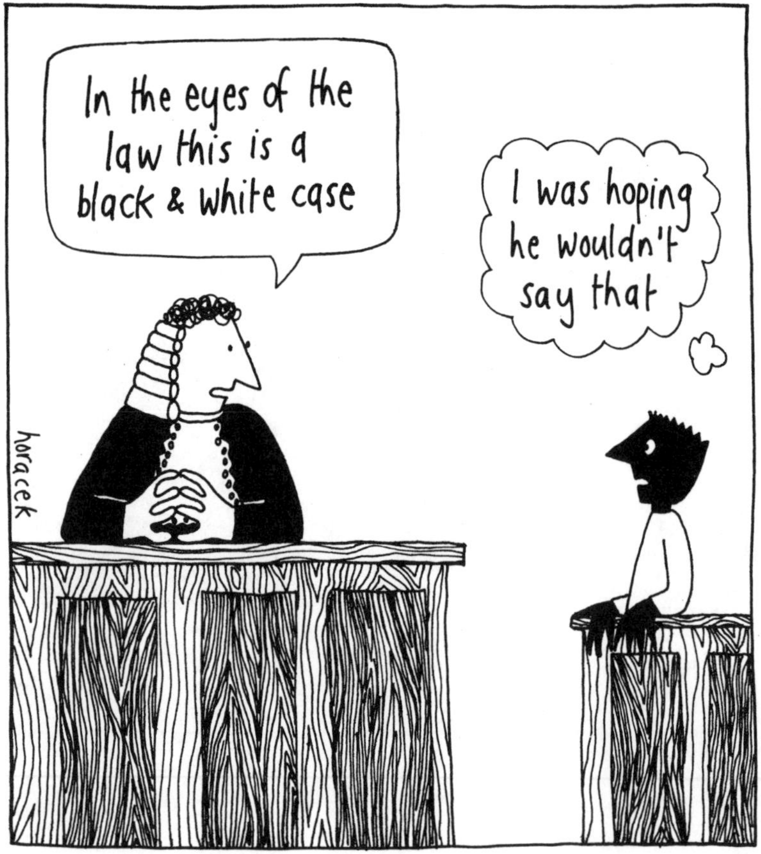
In the eyes of the law this is a black & white case
I was hoping he wouldn't say that
horacek

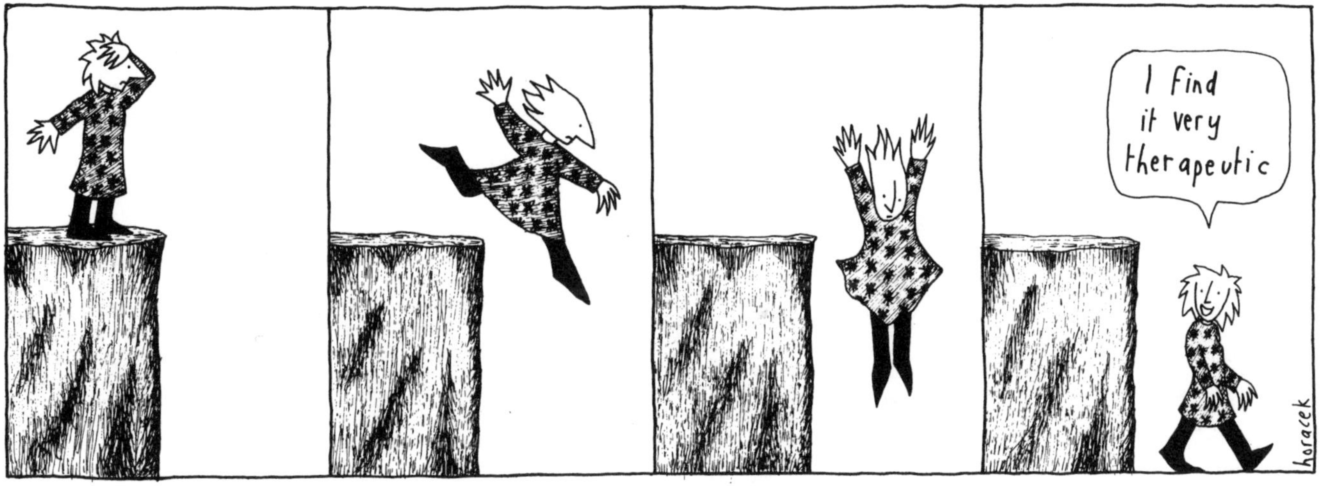
I find it very therapeutic
horacek

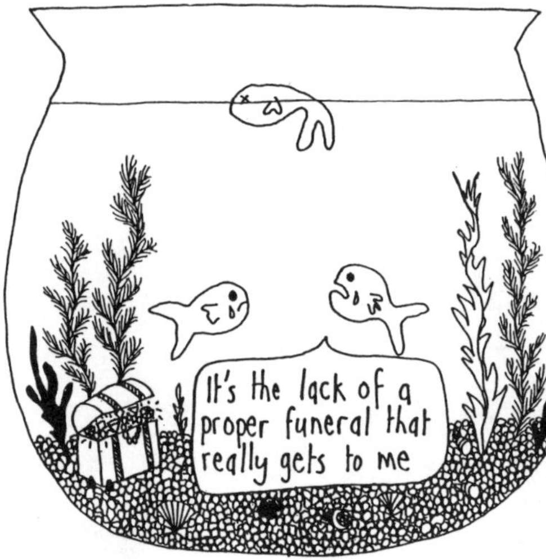
It's the lack of a proper funeral that really gets to me
horacek

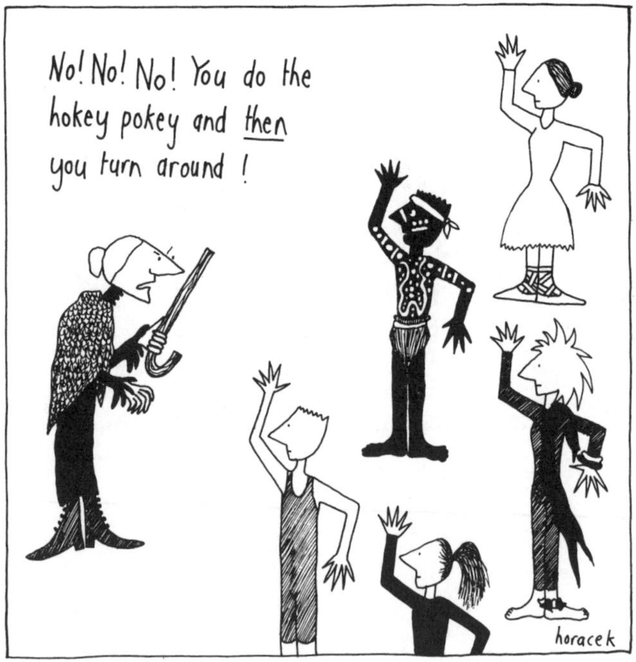
No! No! No! You do the hokey pokey and then you turn around !
horacek

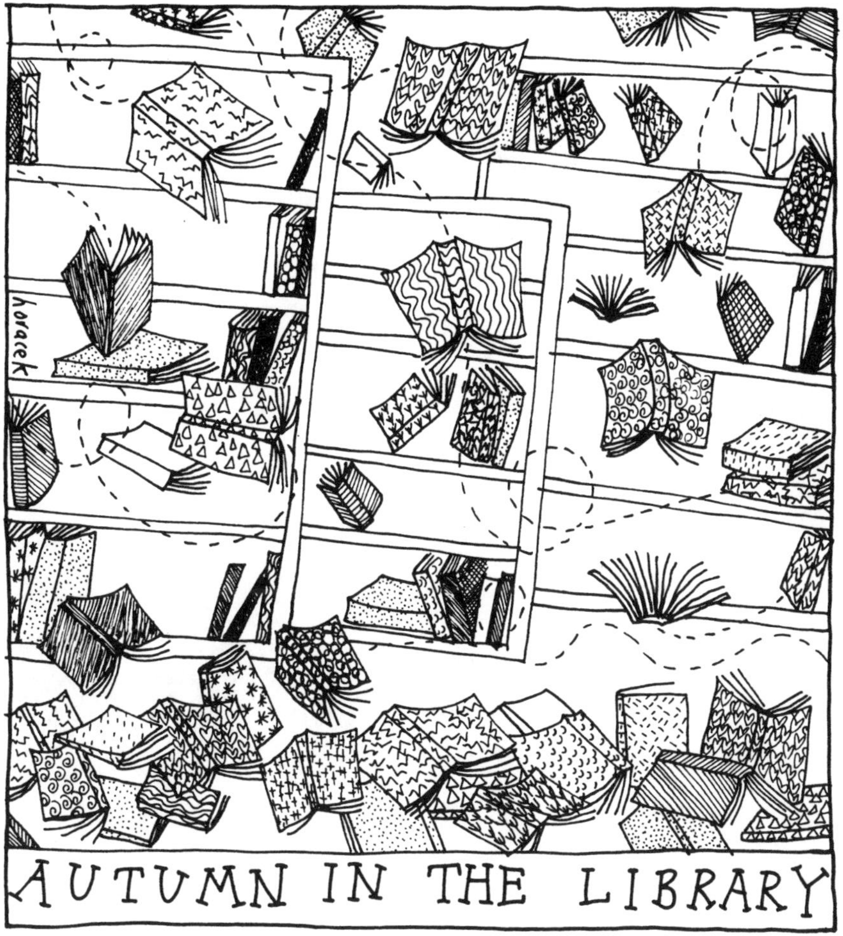
horacek

AUTUMN IN THE LIBRARY

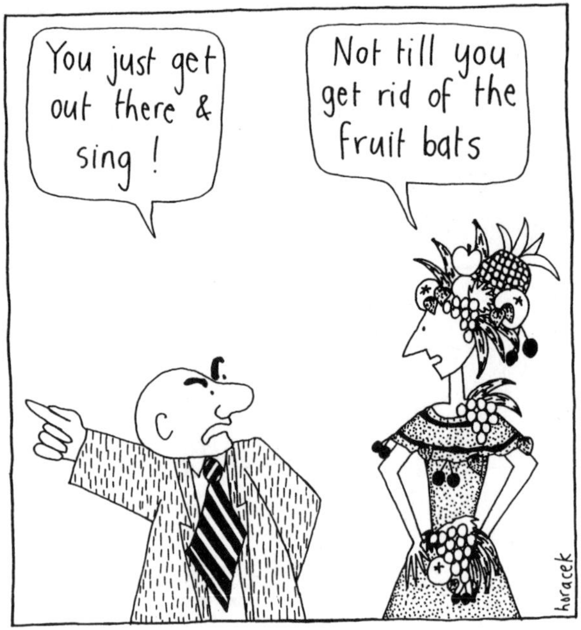
You just get out there & sing !
Not till you get rid of the fruit bats
horacek

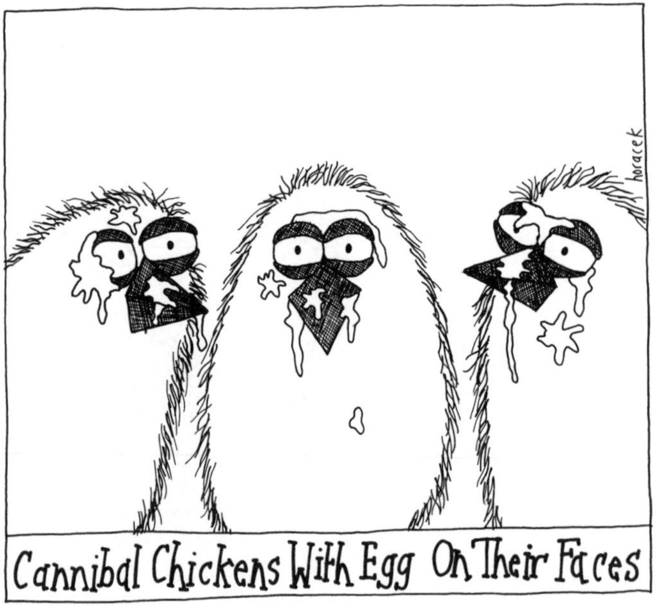
horacek
Cannibal Chickens With Egg On Their Faces

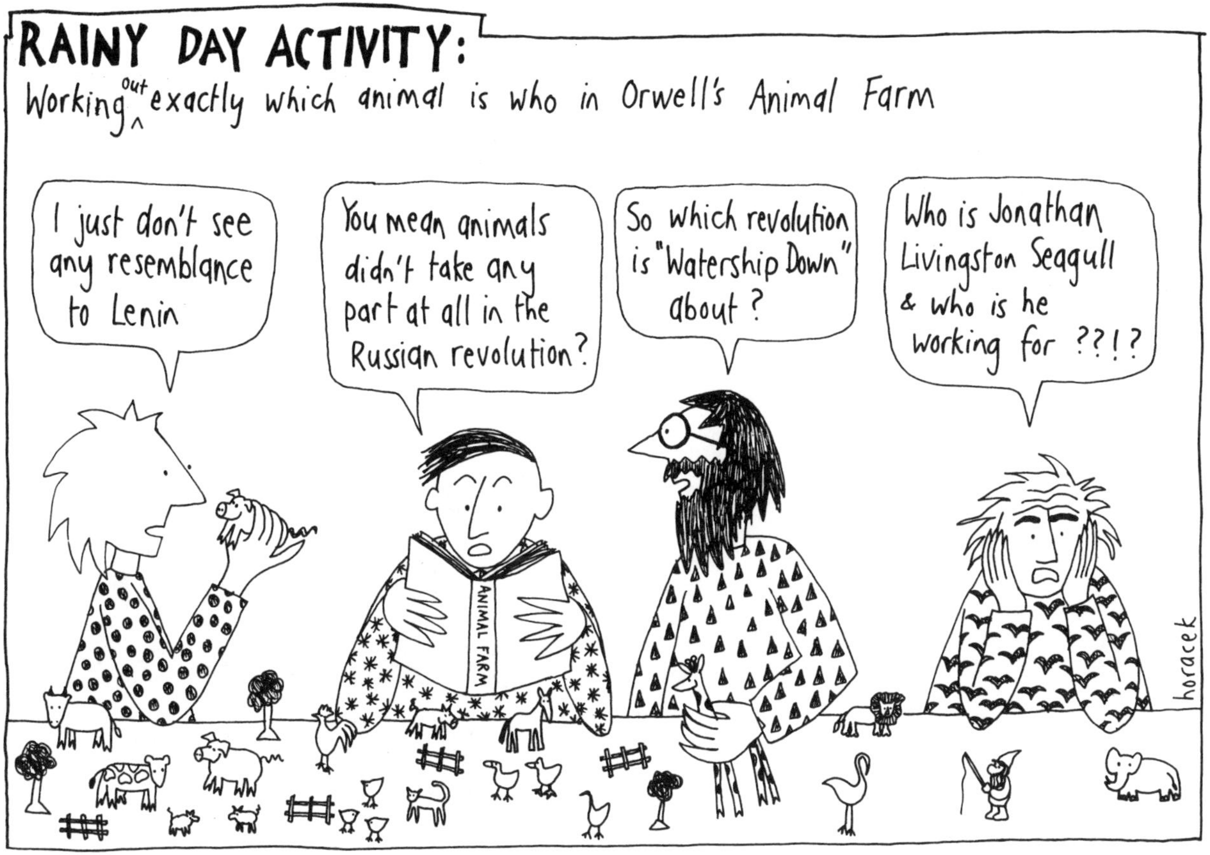
RAINY DAY ACTIVITY:
Working out exactly which animal is who in Orwell's Animal Farm
I just don't see any resemblance to Lenin
You mean animals didn't take any part at all in the Russian revolution?
So which revolution is "Watership Down" about?
Who is Jonathan Livingston Seagull & who is he working for ??!?
ANIMAL FARM
horacek

Take 2 pieces of technology & I'll see you in the morning
horacek

New!
New!
actual size!
Blue Roses!
Mini Cows!
EXTINCT
EXTINCT
EXTINCT
EXTINCT
EXTINCT
EXTINCT
EXTINCT
EXTINCT
EXTINCT
EXTINCT
EXTINCT
horacek

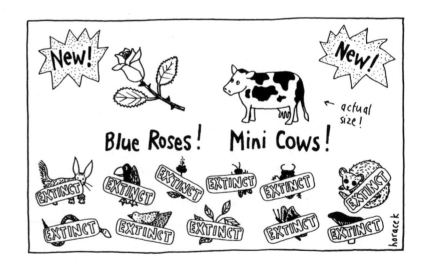

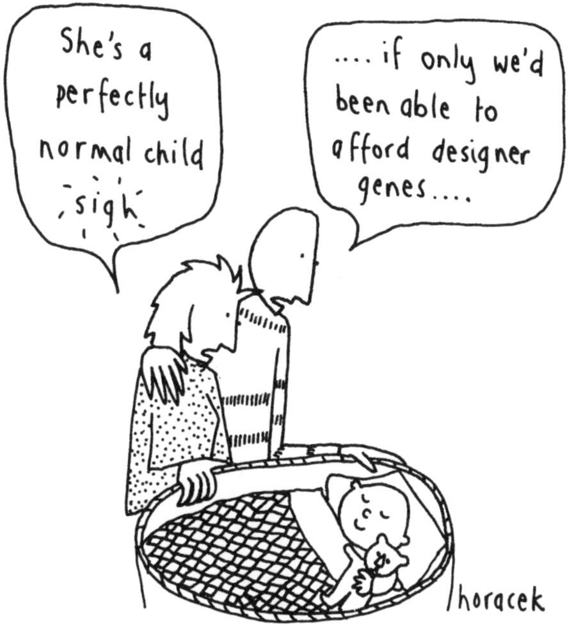
She's a perfectly normal child
sigh
....if only we'd been able to afford designer genes....
horacek

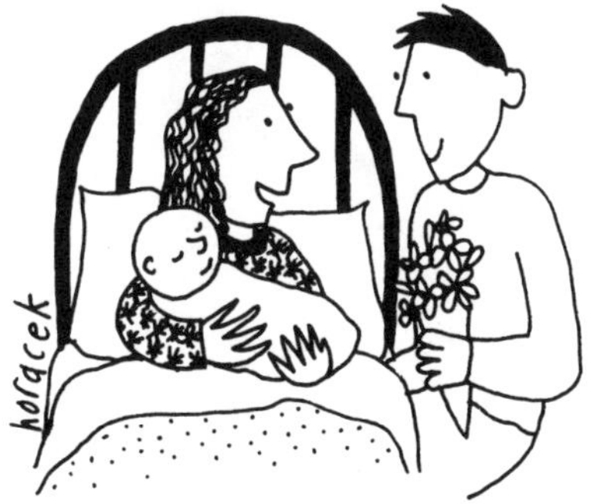
horacek

And he comes with a "free replacement" guarantee in case any faults develop later

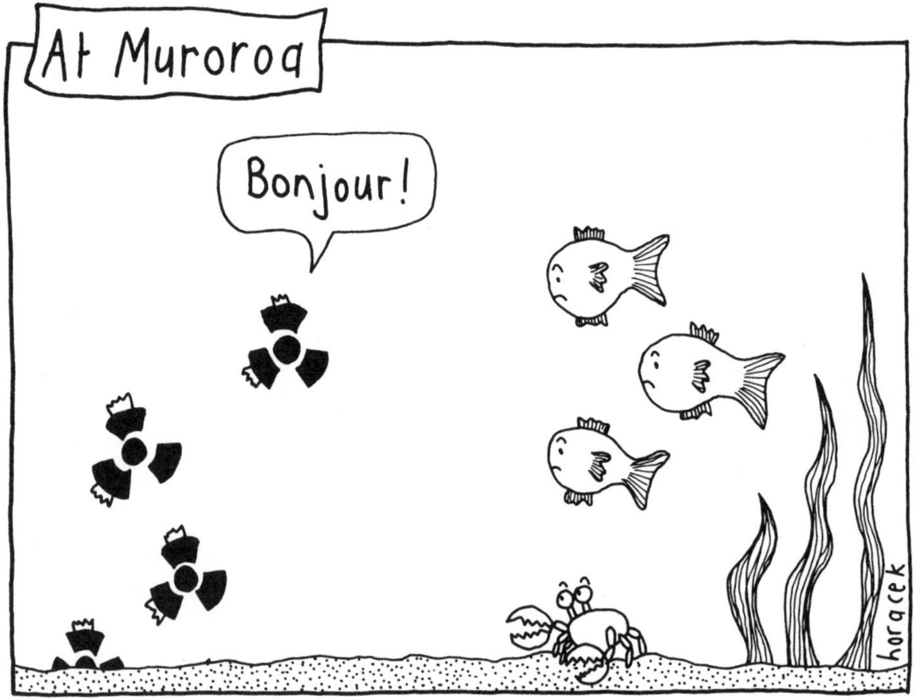
At Muroroa
Bonjour!
horacek

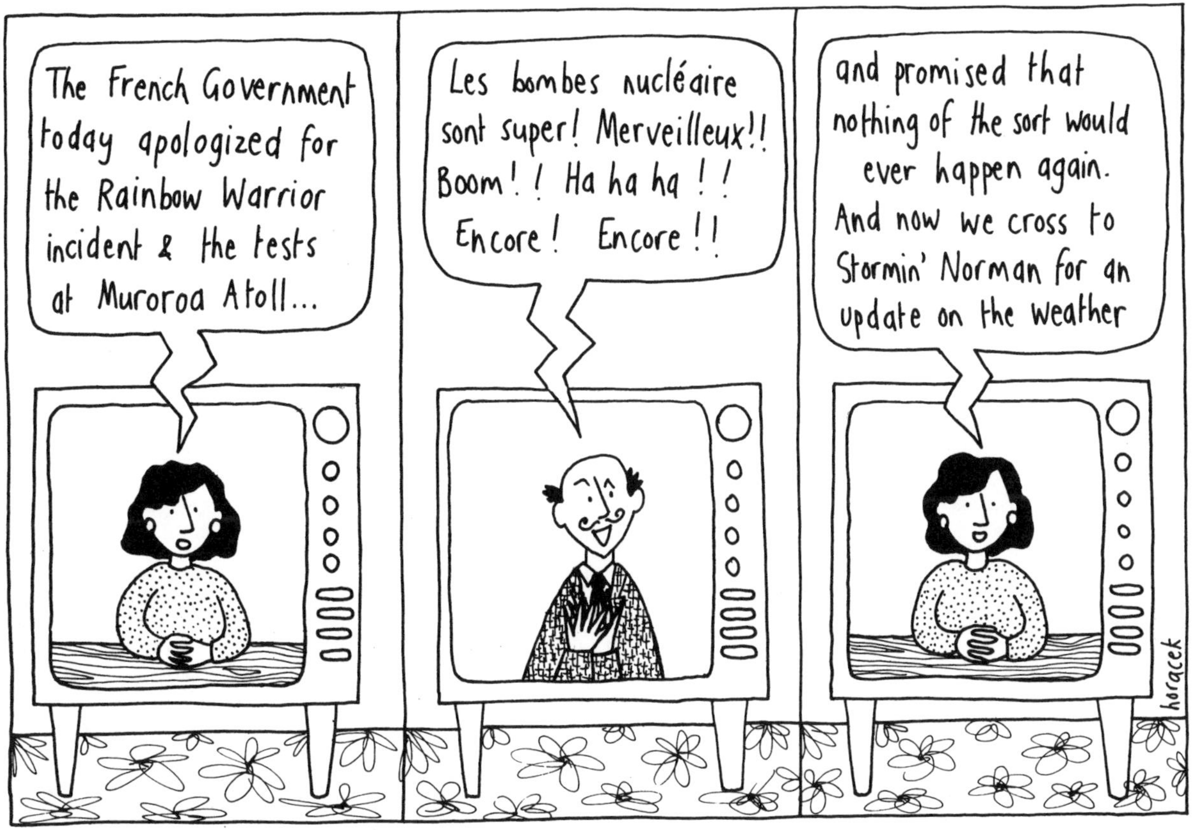
The French Government today apologized for the Rainbow Warrior incident & the tests at Muroroa Atoll...
Les bombes nucléaire sont super! Merveilleux!! Boom!! Ha ha ha!! Encore! Encore!!
and promised that nothing of the sort would ever happen again. And now we cross to Stormin' Norman for an update on the weather
horacek

·ATOMIC·THEORY·A·LA·MODE·
electron
proton
N
+
neutron
futon
horacek

The Seventies Revival
This is the darning of the Age of Aquarius
horacek

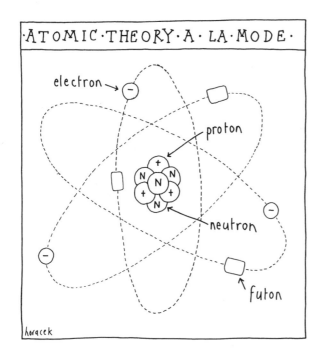

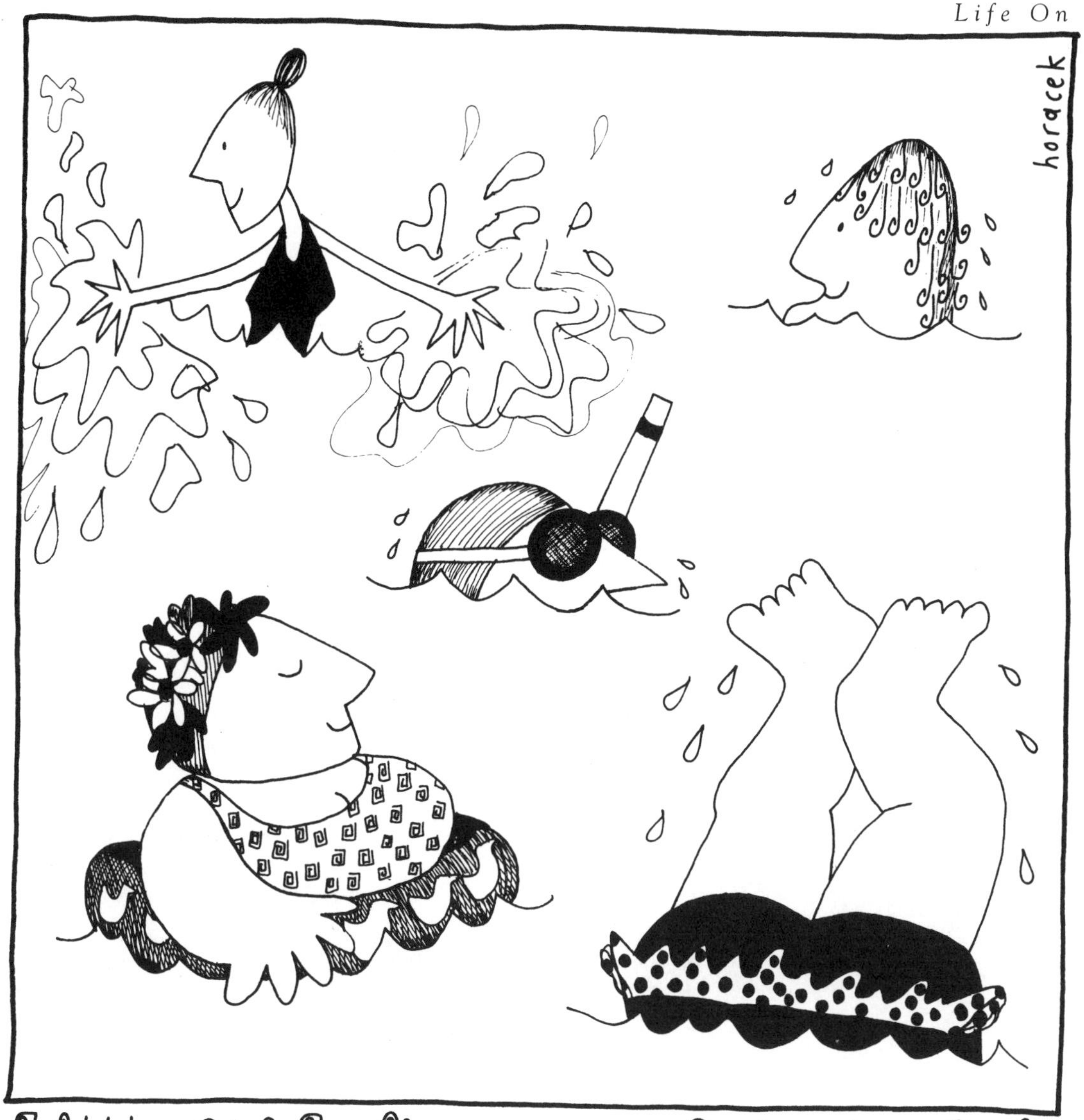
horacek

Little Old Ladies at the Swimming Pool

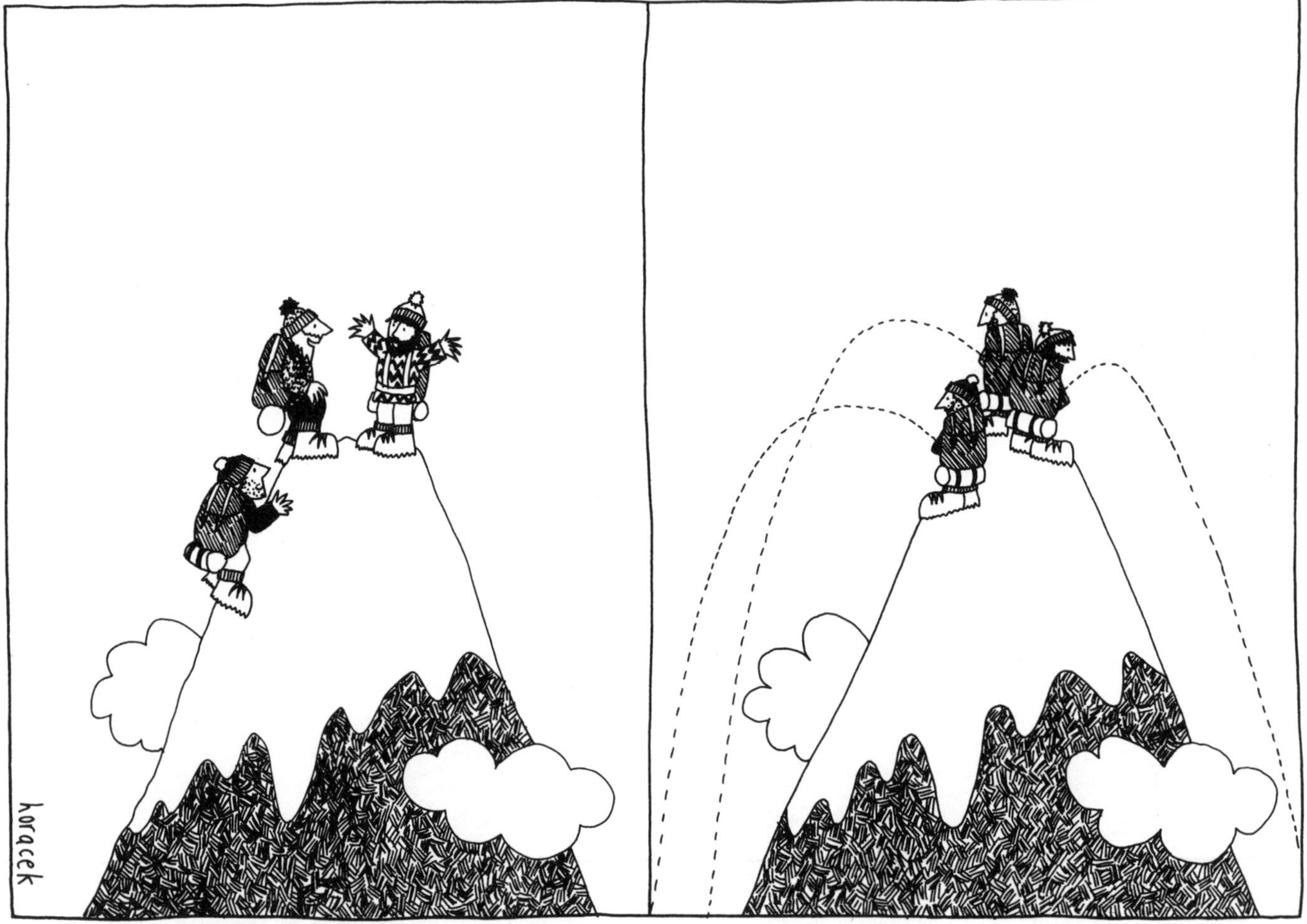
horacek

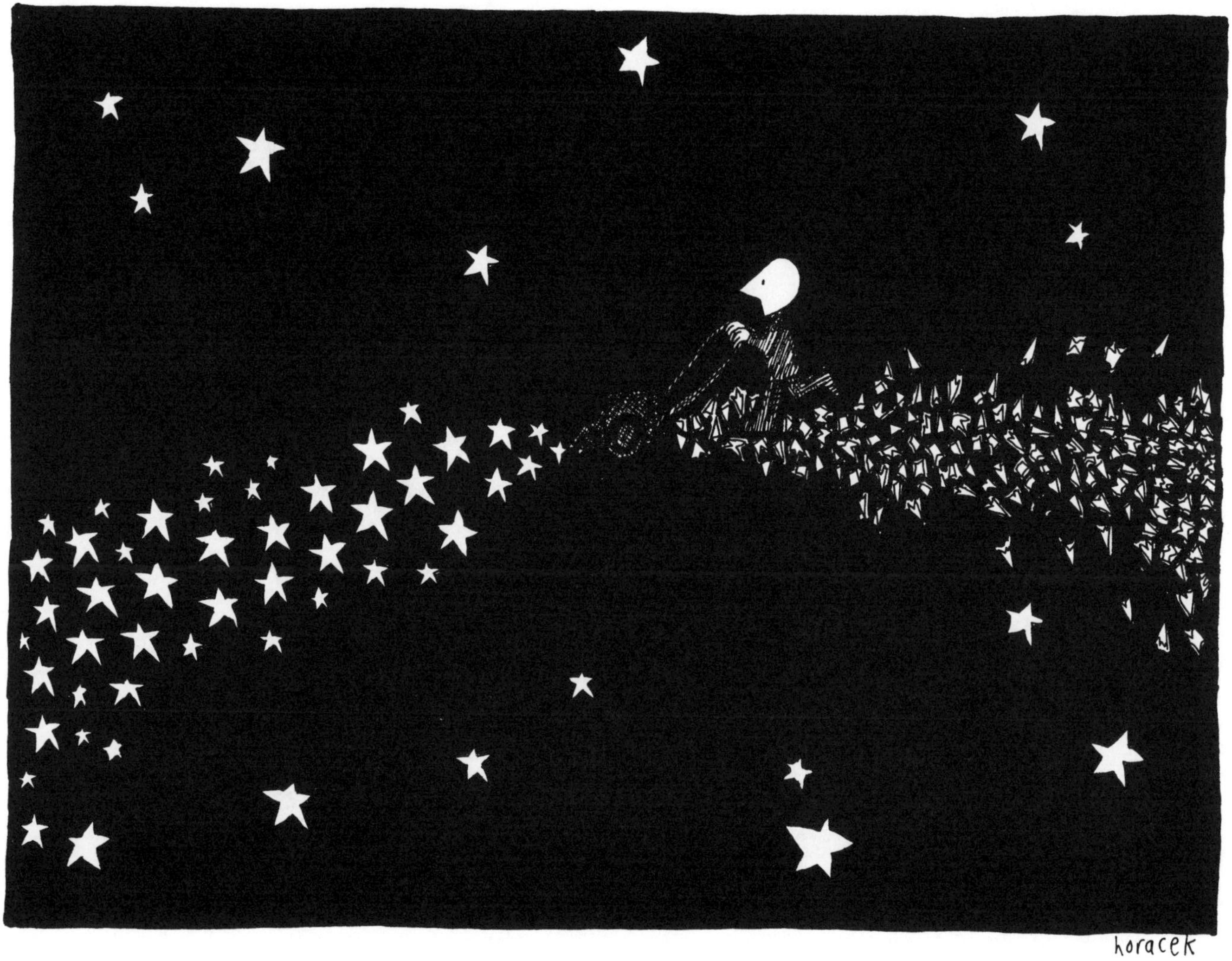
horacek

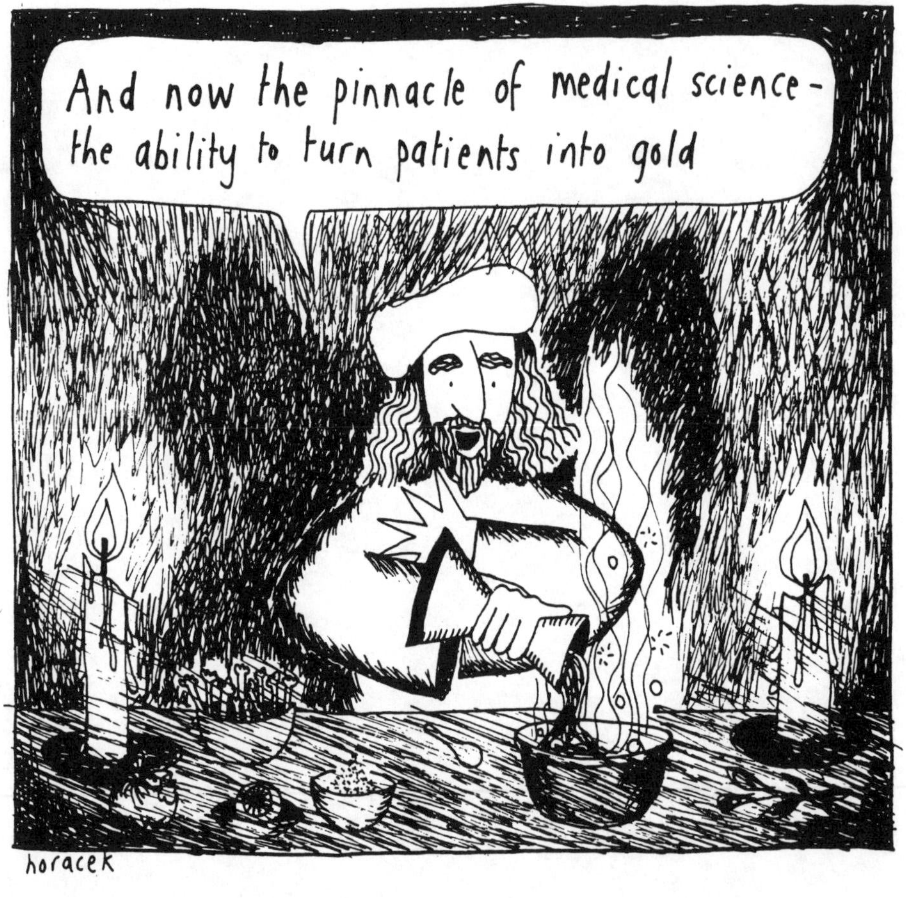
And now the pinnacle of medical science -
the ability to turn patients into gold
horacek

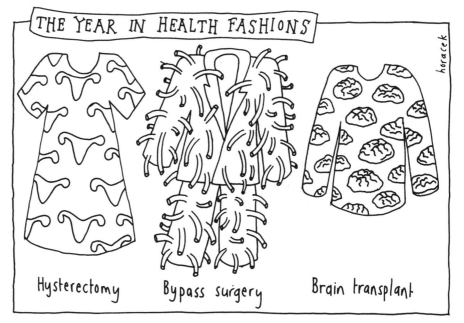

THE YEAR IN HEALTH FASHIONS

Hysterectomy   Bypass surgery   Brain transplant

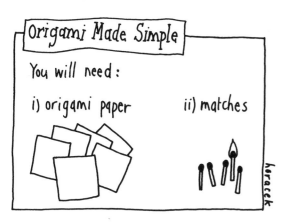

Origami Made Simple

You will need:

i) origami paper   ii) matches

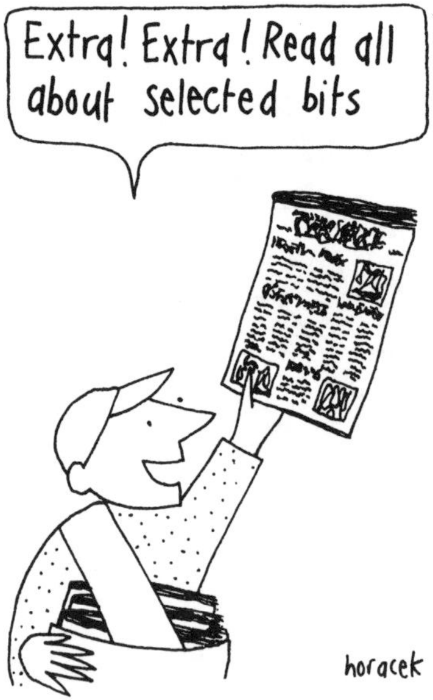
Extra! Extra! Read all about selected bits
horacek

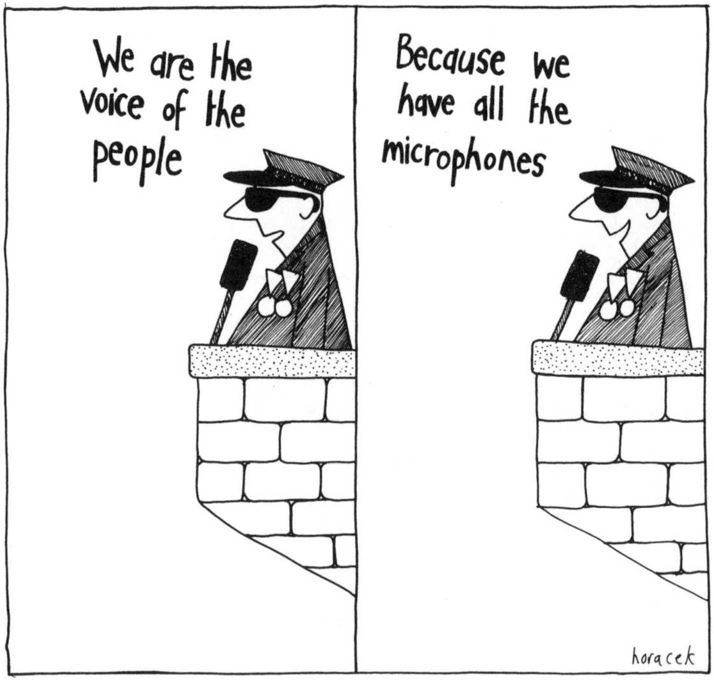
We are the voice of the people
Because we have all the microphones
horacek

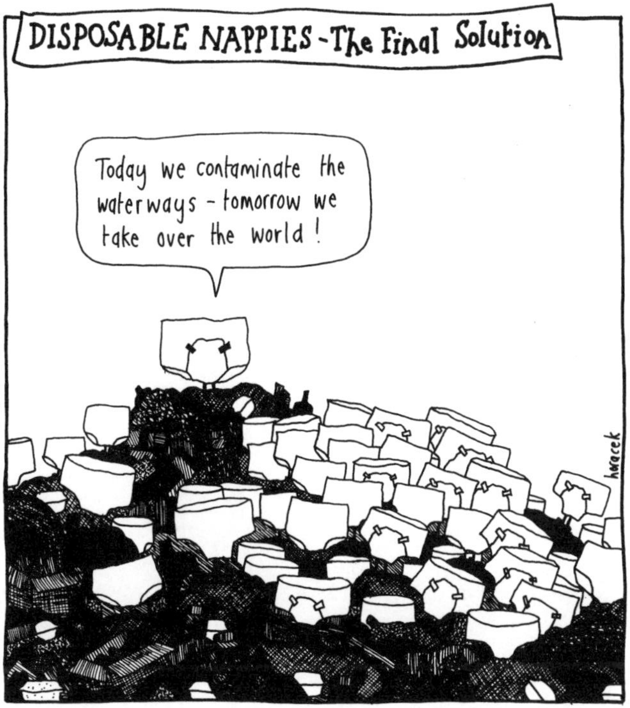
DISPOSABLE NAPPIES - The Final Solution
Today we contaminate the waterways - tomorrow we take over the world!
horacek

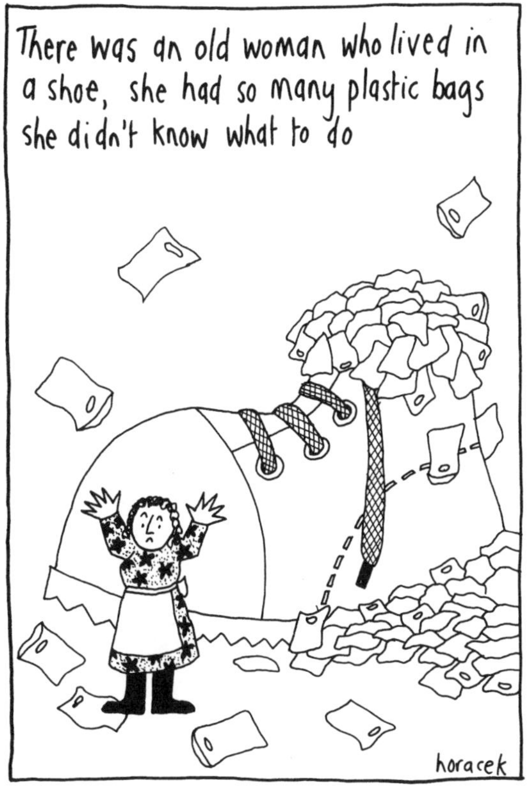
There was an old woman who lived in a shoe, she had so many plastic bags she didn't know what to do
horacek

PATRIARCHY RULES
No 1 Non-Provocative Dressing
Providing you also lock yourself in a bank vault, this outfit is a 55% sure way to avoid being accused of inviting rape
No 2 Non-Provocative Behaviour
horacek
INVISIBILITY or NON-EXISTENCE
Choose whichever is easier and/or more satisfying to you

Don't talk to strangers
In fact, don't talk to anyone
Just don't talk at all

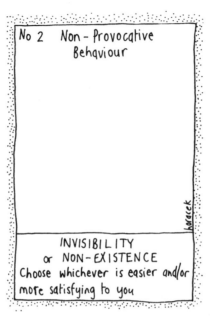

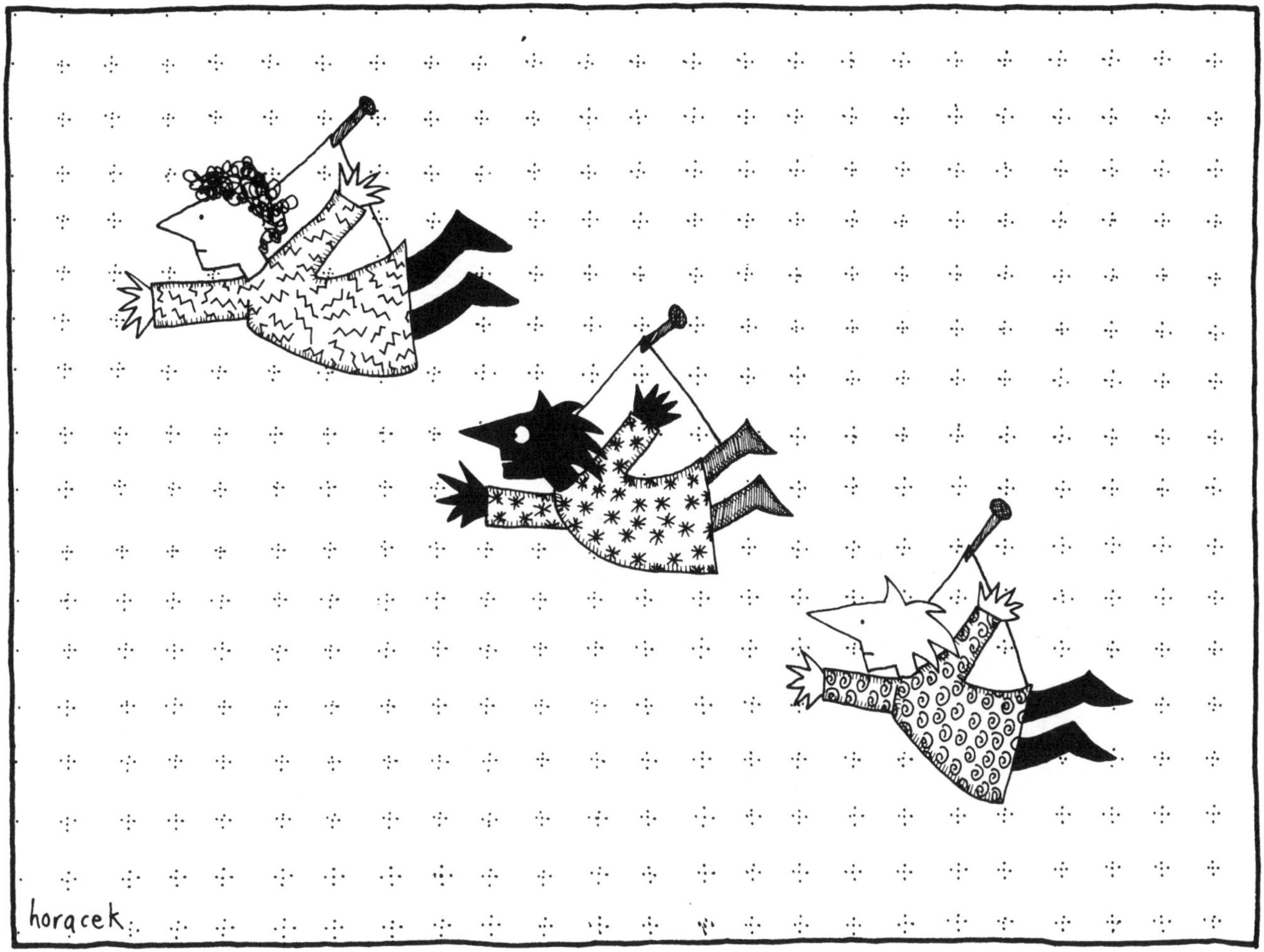
horacek

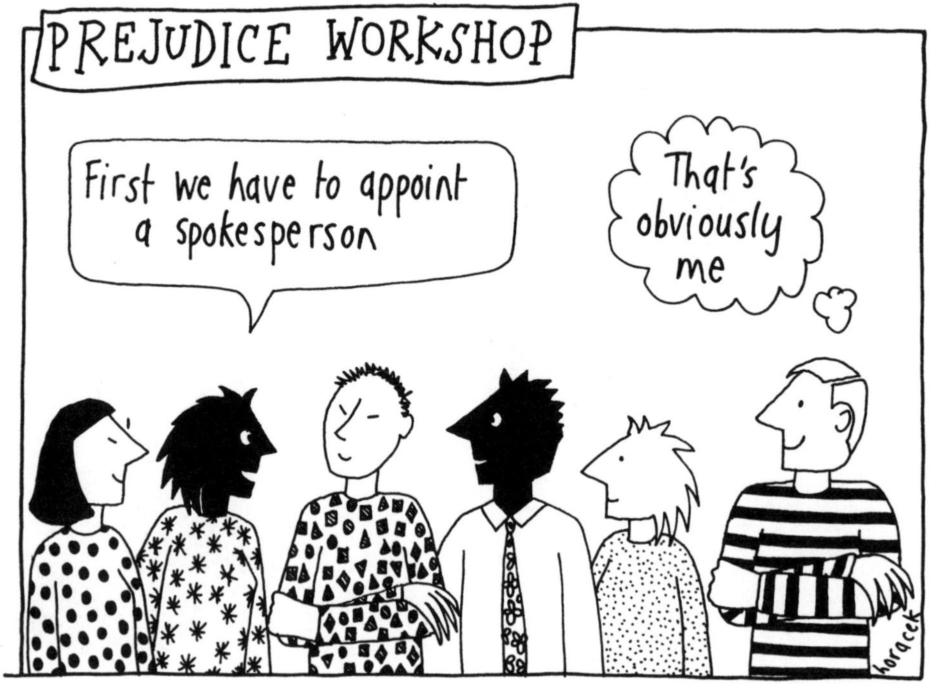
PREJUDICE WORKSHOP
First we have to appoint a spokesperson
That's obviously me
horacek

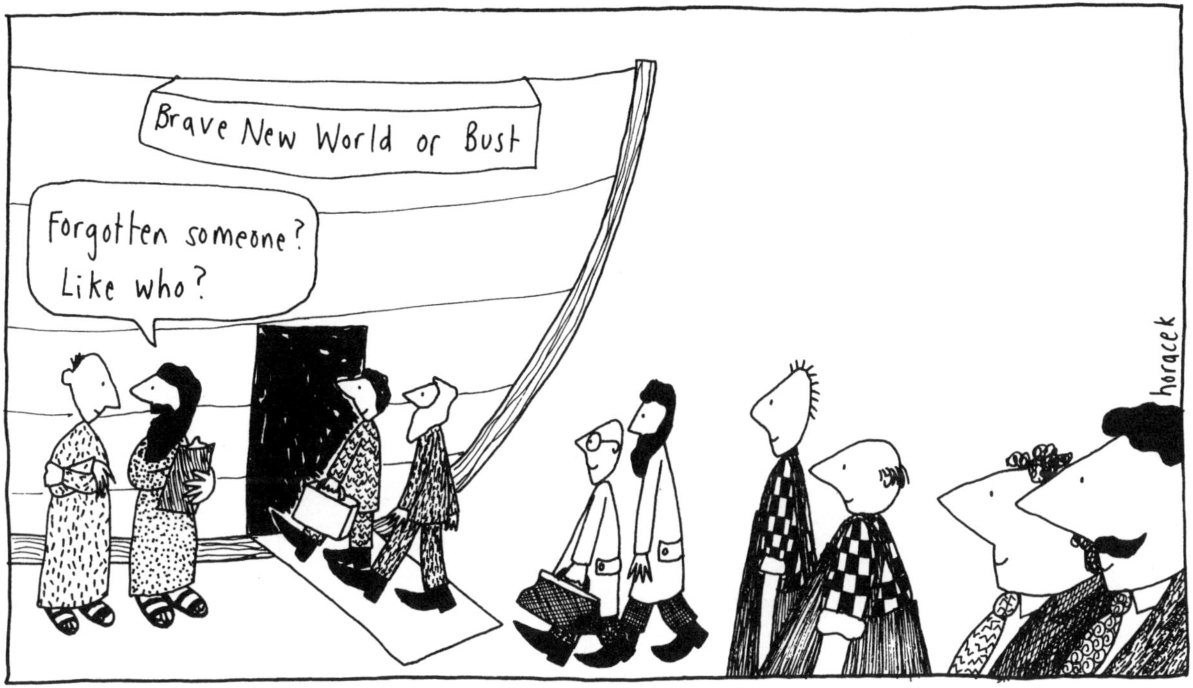
Brave New World or Bust
Forgotten someone? Like who?
horacek

I'll have the latest
Menu
horacek

SIGNIFICANT PHASES IN THE SEARCH FOR THE ANSWER
The existential phase
The postmodern phase
The yuppie phase
The new age phase
horacek

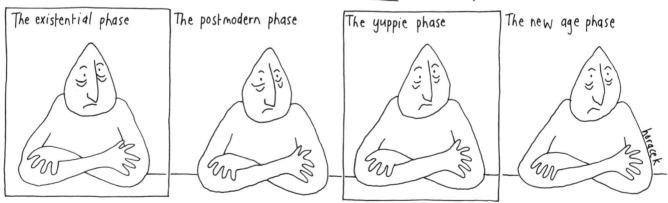

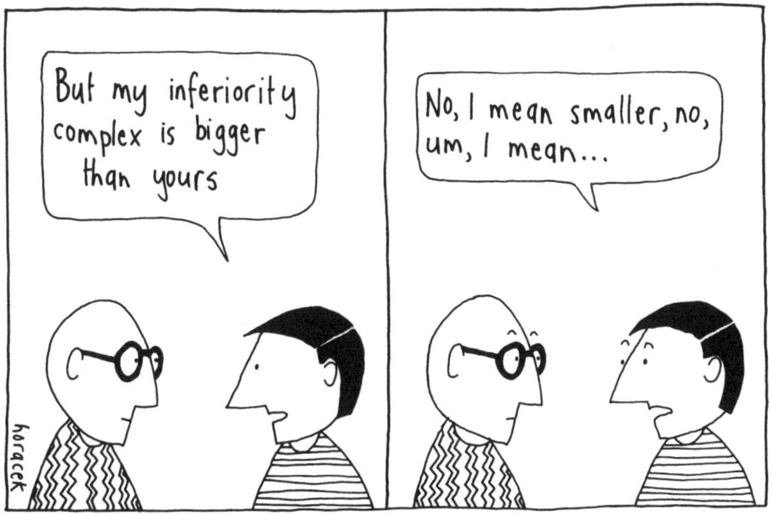
But my inferiority complex is bigger than yours
No, I mean smaller, no, um, I mean...
horacek

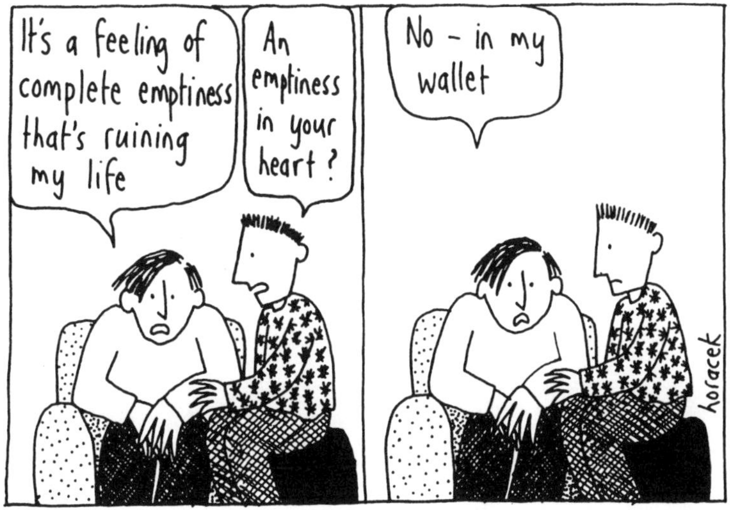
It's a feeling of complete emptiness that's ruining my life
An emptiness in your heart?
No - in my wallet
horacek

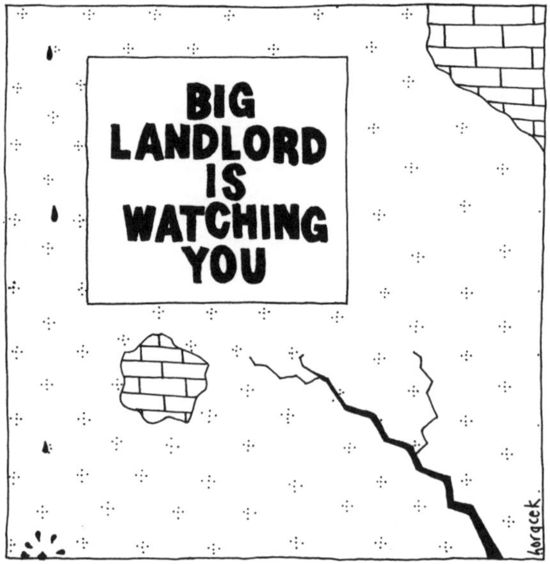
BIG LANDLORD IS WATCHING YOU
horacek

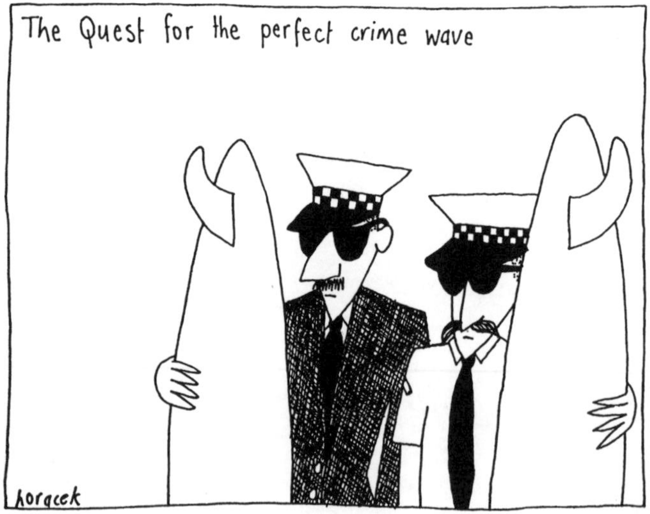
The Quest for the perfect crime wave
horacek

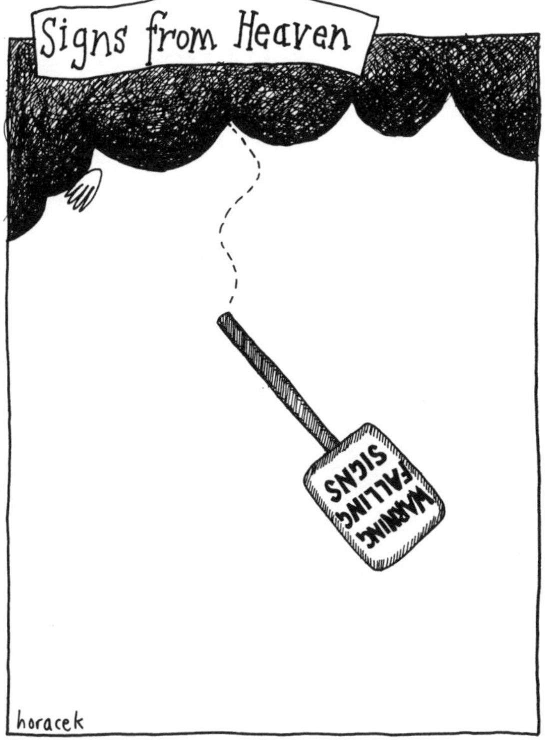
Signs from Heaven
WARNING FALLING SIGNS
horacek

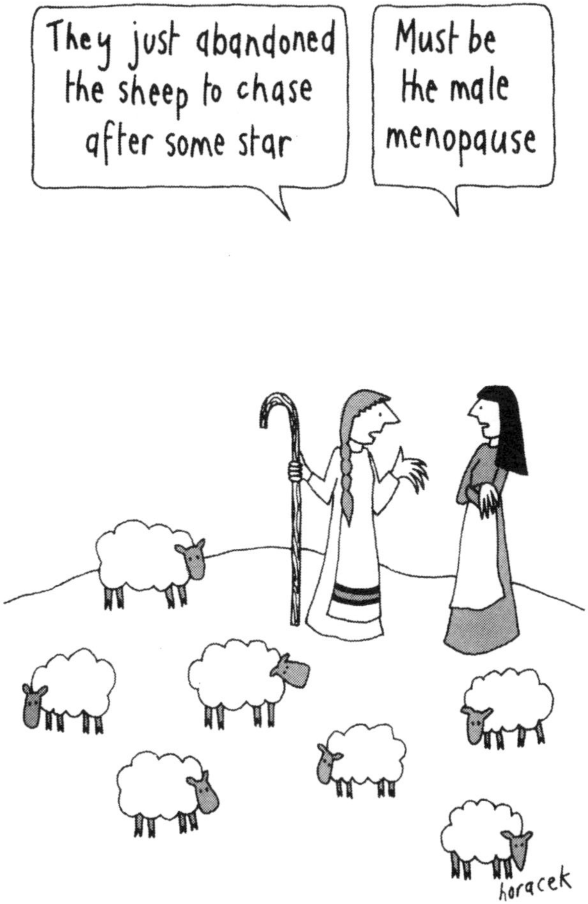
They just abandoned the sheep to chase after some star
Must be the male menopause
horacek

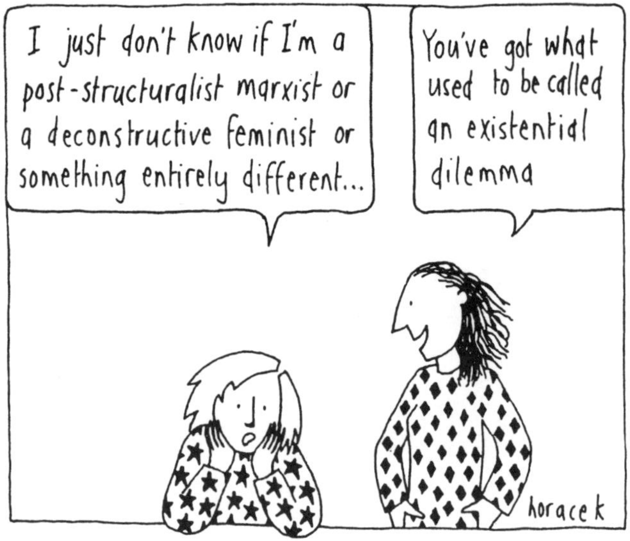
I just don't know if I'm a post-structuralist marxist or a deconstructive feminist or something entirely different...
You've got what used to be called an existential dilemma
horacek

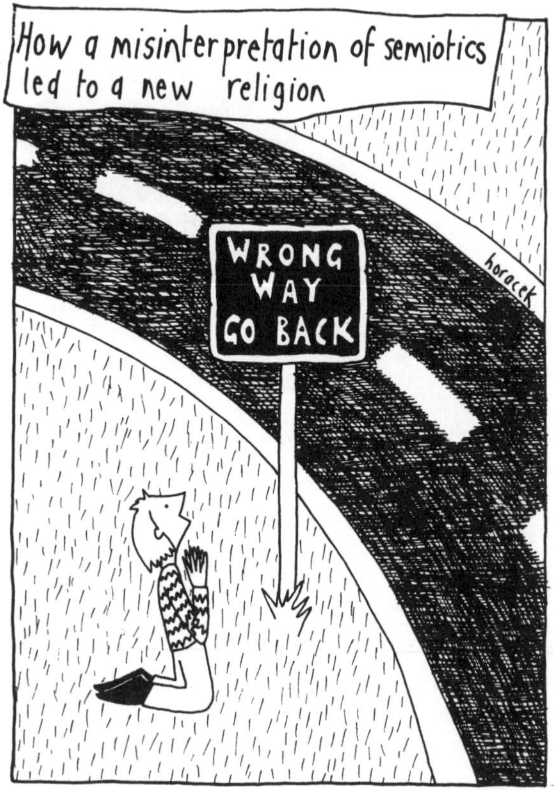
How a misinterpretation of semiotics led to a new religion
WRONG WAY GO BACK
horacek

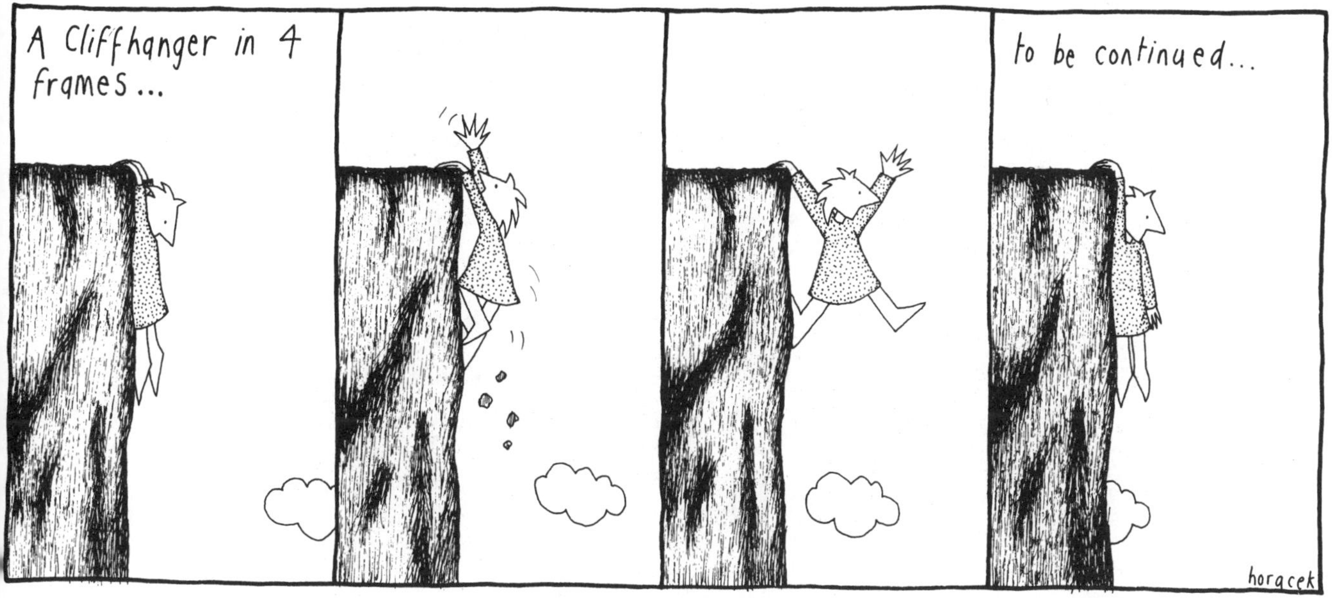
A Cliffhanger in 4 frames...
to be continued...
horacek

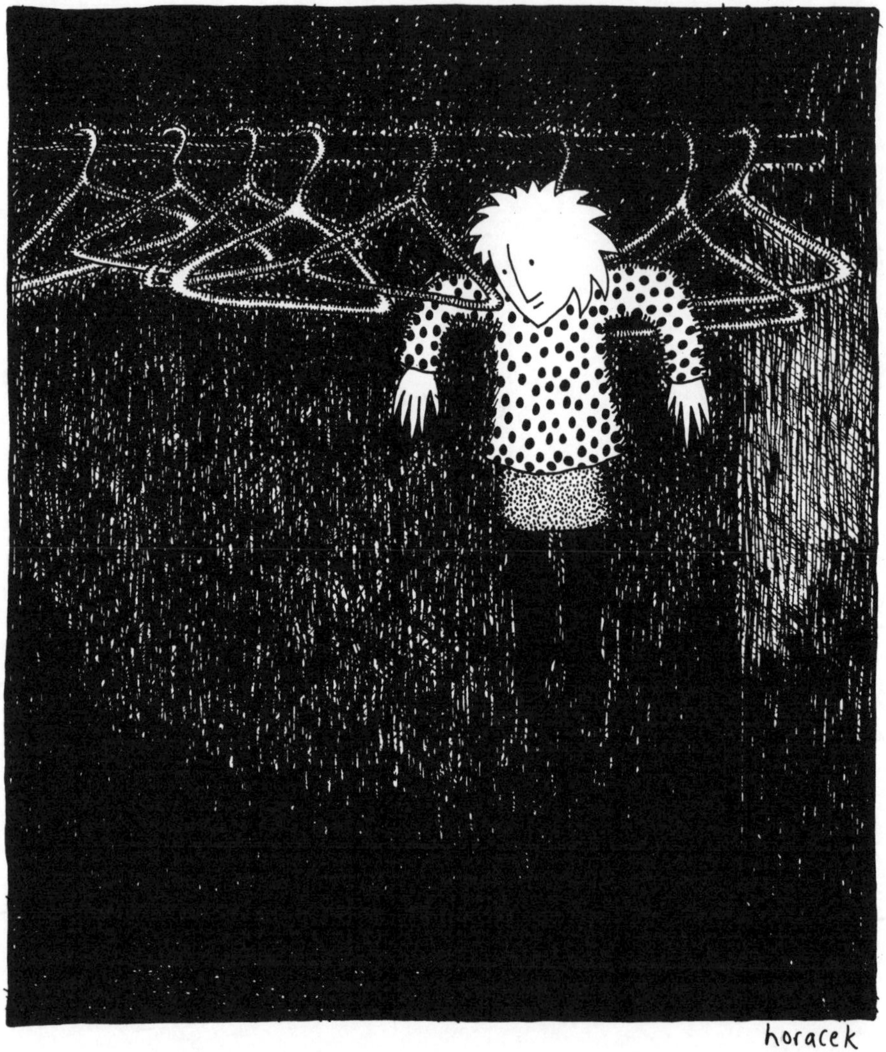
horacek

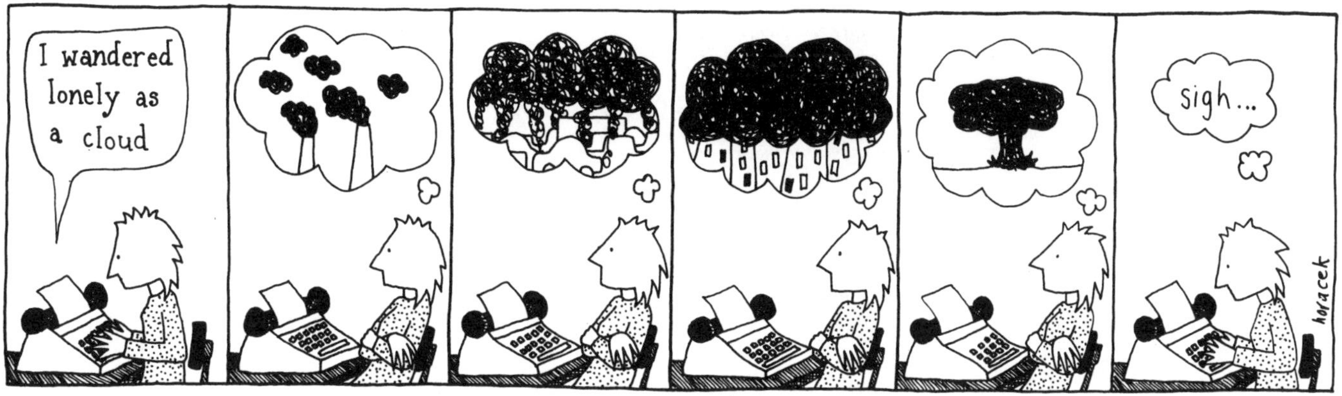
I wandered lonely as a cloud
sigh...
horacek

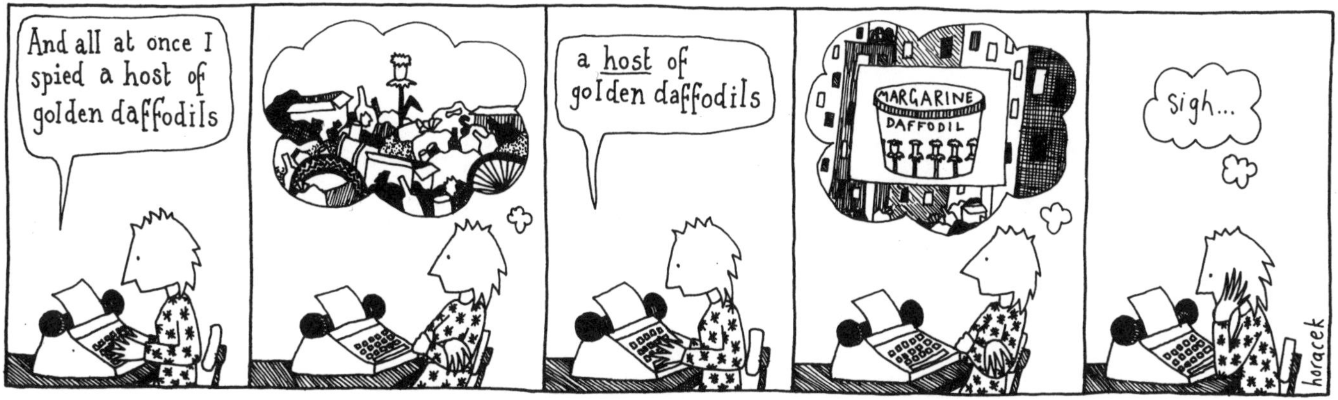
And all at once I spied a host of golden daffodils
a host of golden daffodils
MARGARINE
DAFFODIL
sigh...
horacek

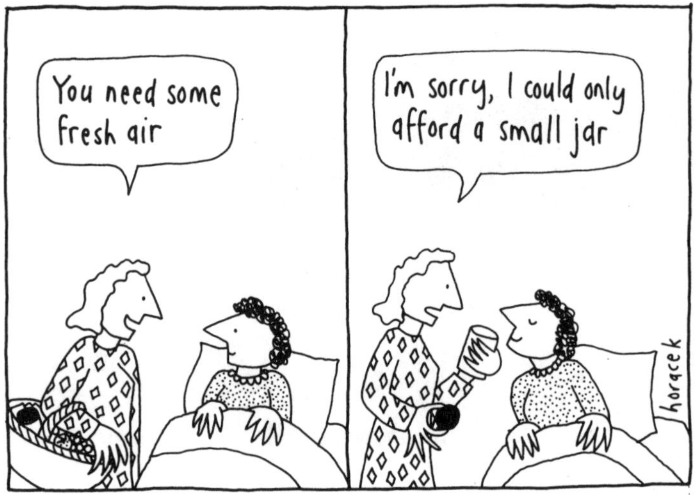
You need some fresh air
I'm sorry, I could only afford a small jar
horacek

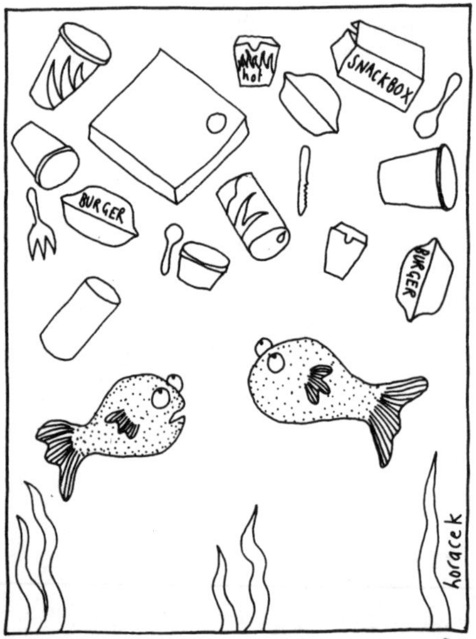
SNACKBOX
hot
BURGER
BURGER
horacek
Did you order take aways?

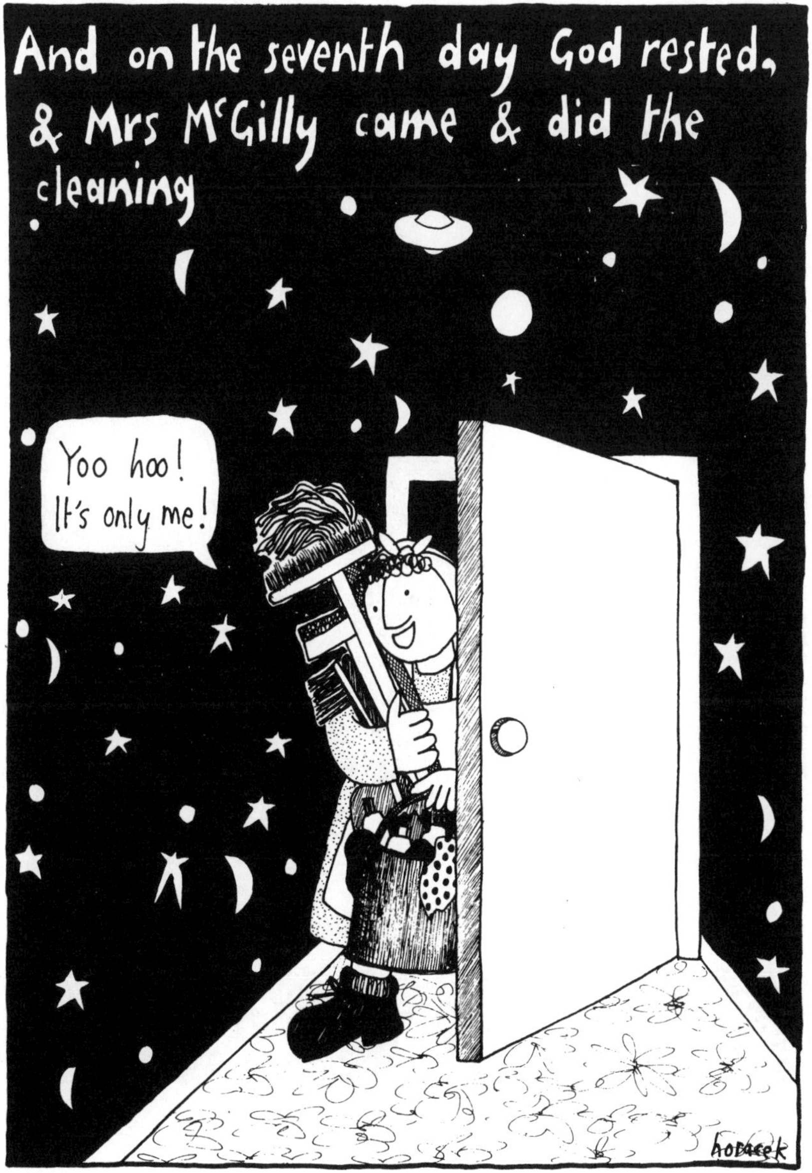
And on the seventh day God rested, & Mrs McGilly came & did the cleaning
Yoo hoo! It's only me!
horacek

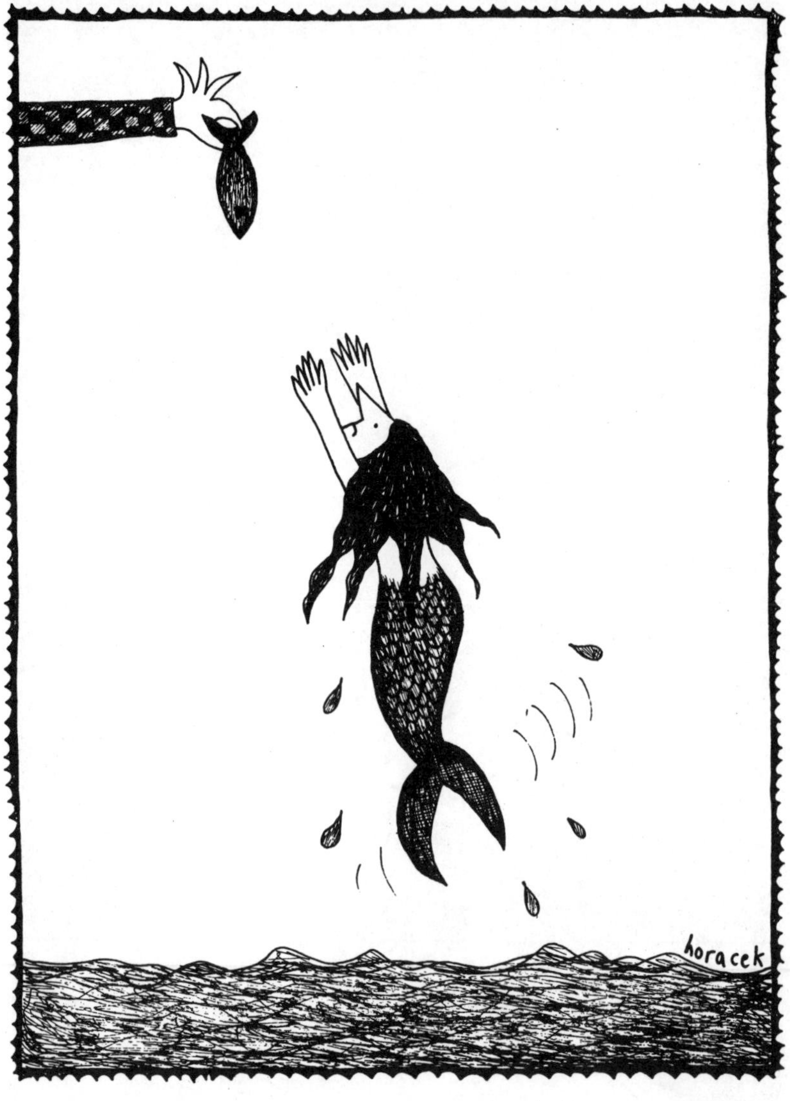
horacek

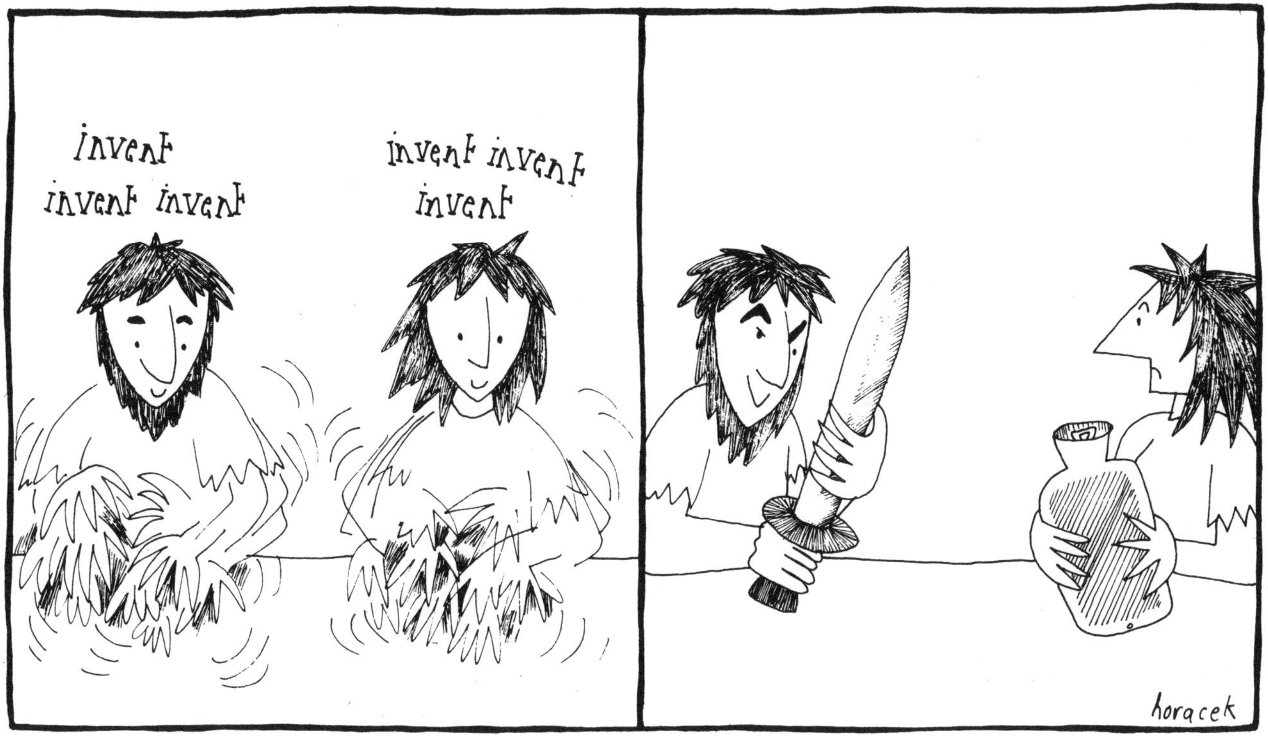
invent
invent invent
invent invent
invent
horacek

The idea of evolution as progress towards increasing perfection has long been discounted by enlightened thinkers. Now read on...

LESSON ONE

The Evolution of the Cotton Bud

INVERTEBRATE Stage 1

Amoebic State
'The Cotton Ball'

INVERTEBRATE Stage 2

Exo - Skeleton
'The Tampon'

VERTEBRATE

Internal Spine
'The Cotton Bud'

horacek

So, although tampons are lower on the evolutionary scale than cotton buds, they cost fifty times more, in the same way as crayfish costs more than flake.

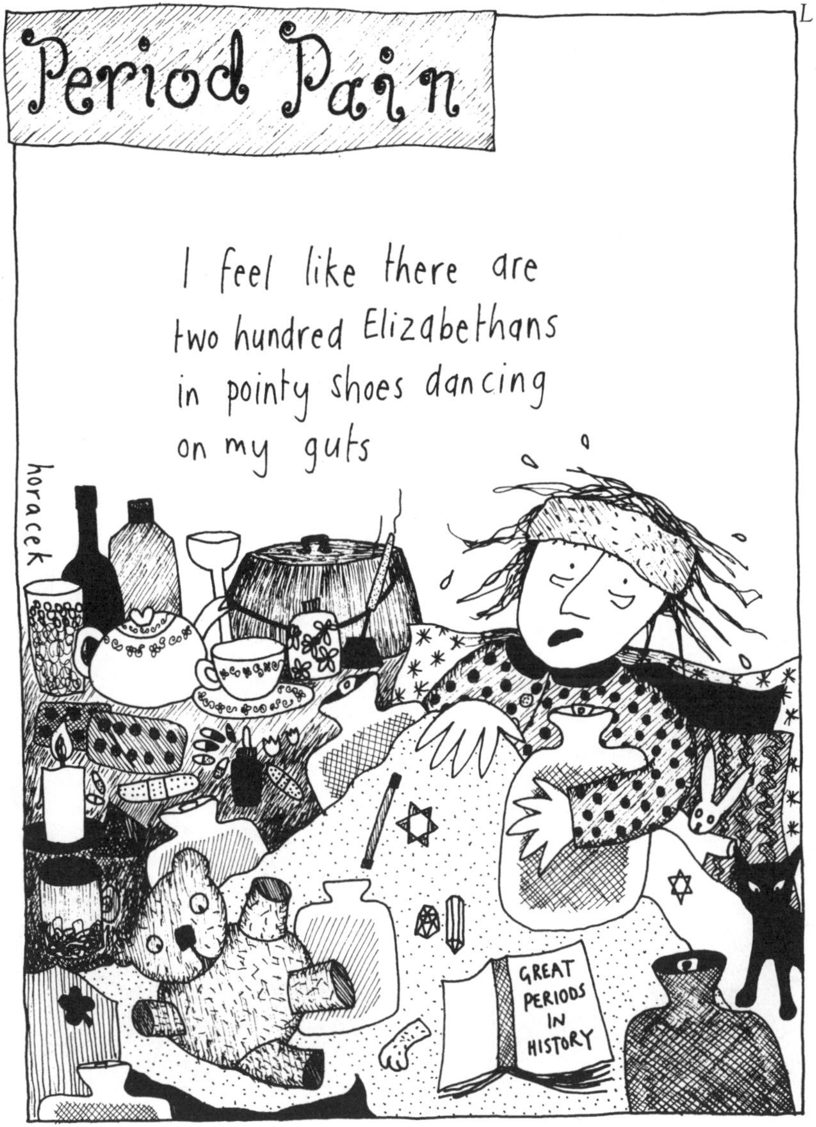
Period Pain
I feel like there are two hundred Elizabethans in pointy shoes dancing on my guts
horacek
GREAT PERIODS IN HISTORY

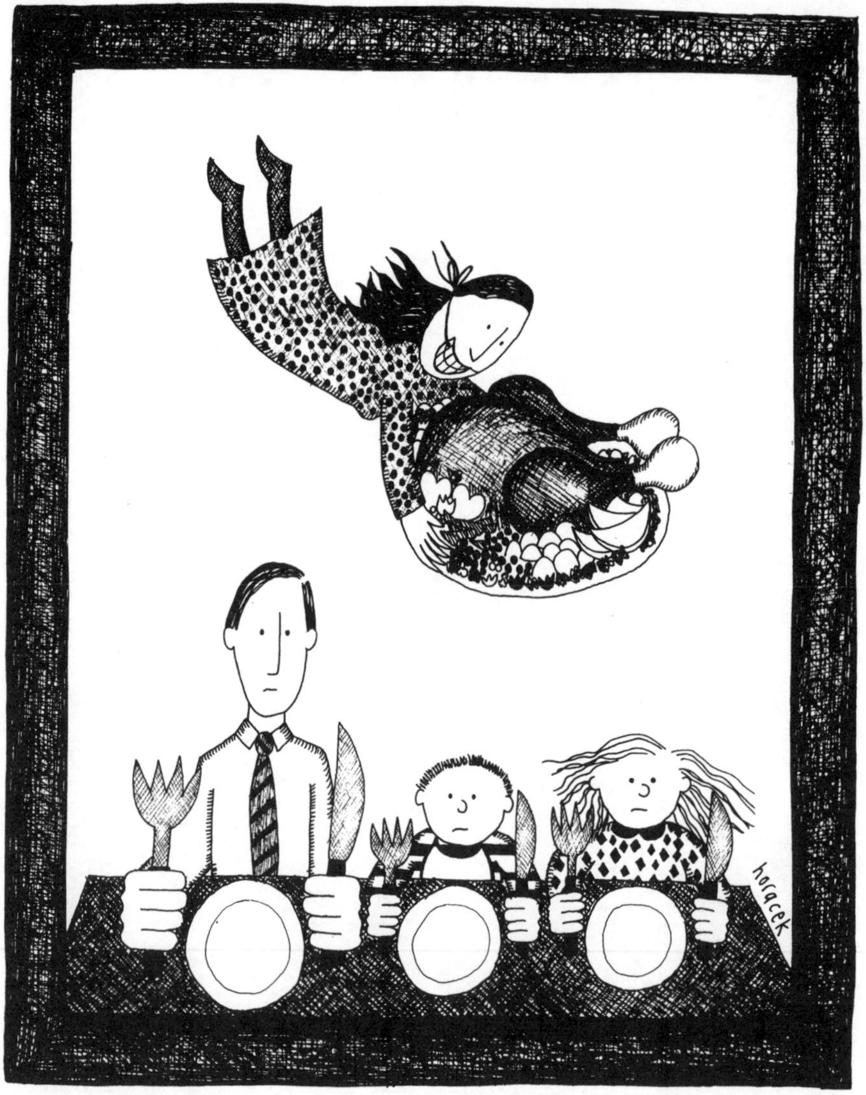
horacek

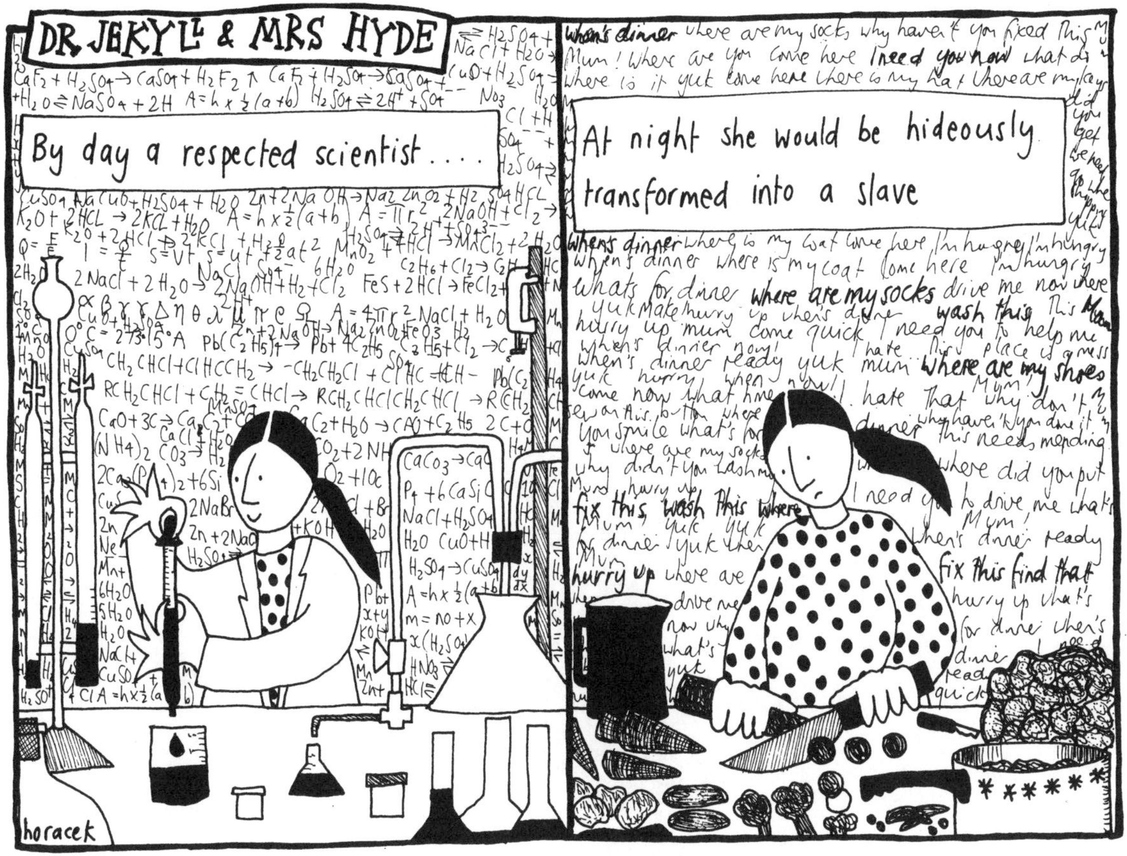
DR. JEKYLL & MRS HYDE
By day a respected scientist....
At night she would be hideously transformed into a slave
horacek

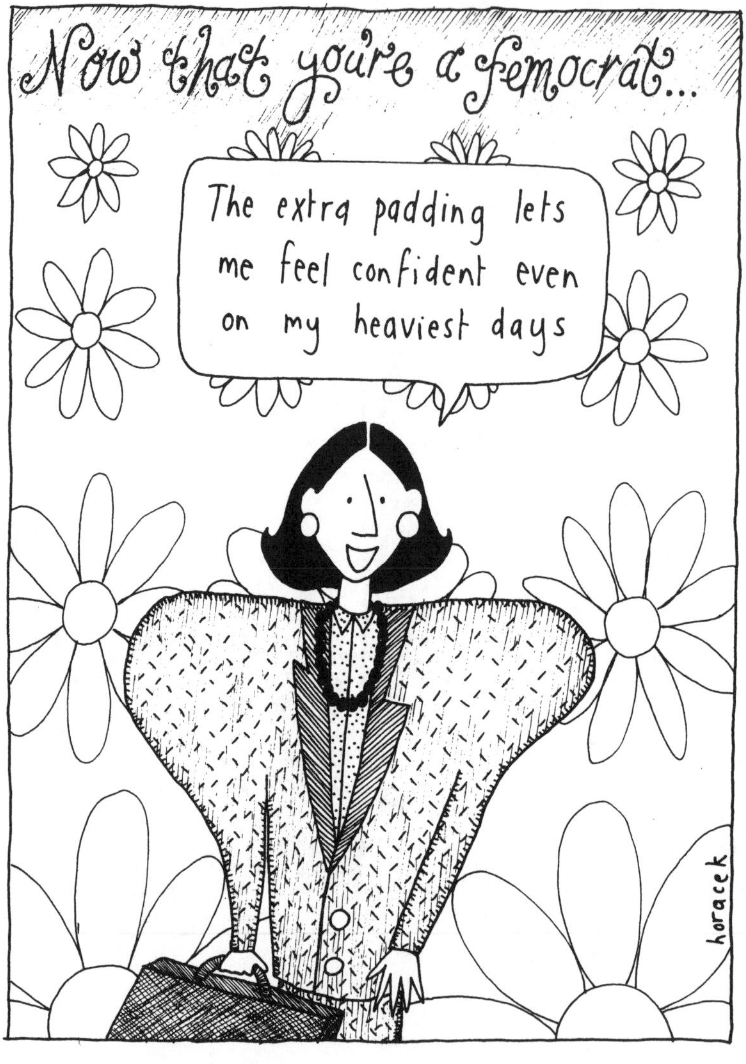
Now that you're a femocrat...
The extra padding lets me feel confident even on my heaviest days
horacek

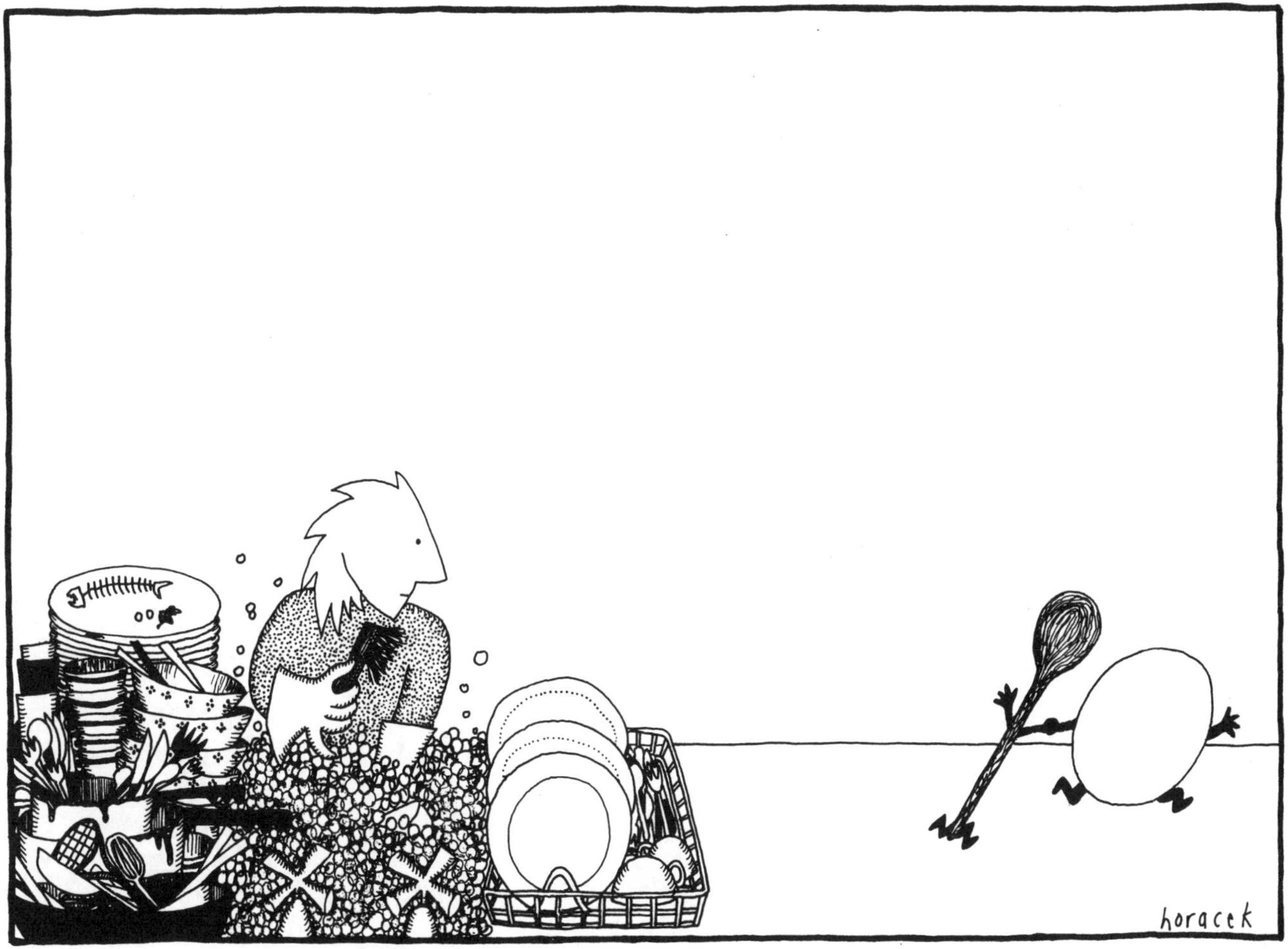
horacek

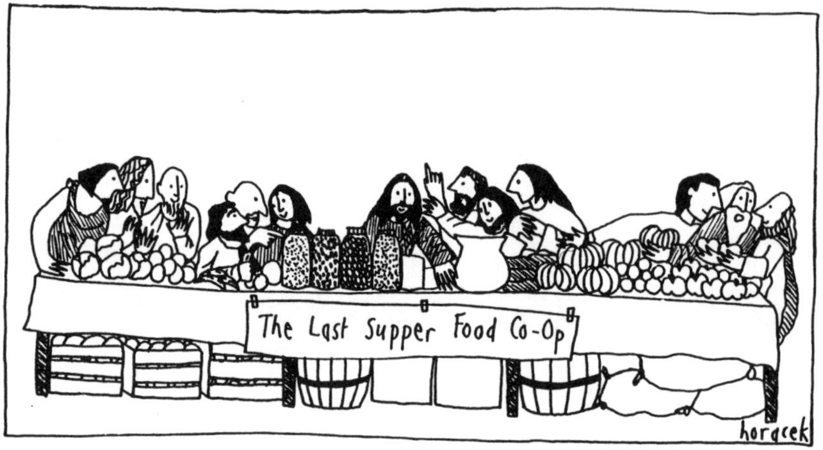
The Last Supper Food Co-Op
horacek

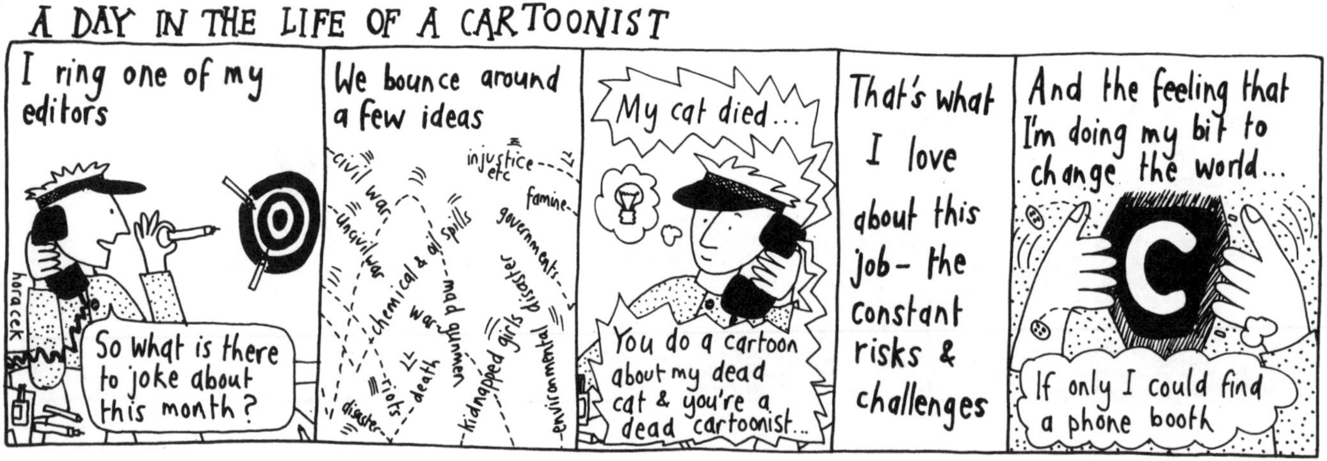
A DAY IN THE LIFE OF A CARTOONIST
I ring one of my editors
horacek
So what is there to joke about this month?
We bounce around a few ideas
civil war
Uncivil war
chemical & oil spills
war
mad gunmen
injustice etc
famine
governments
disaster
kidnapped girls
environmental
riots
death
disaster
My cat died...
You do a cartoon about my dead cat & you're a dead cartoonist...
That's what I love about this job - the constant risks & challenges
And the feeling that I'm doing my bit to change the world...
C
If only I could find a phone booth

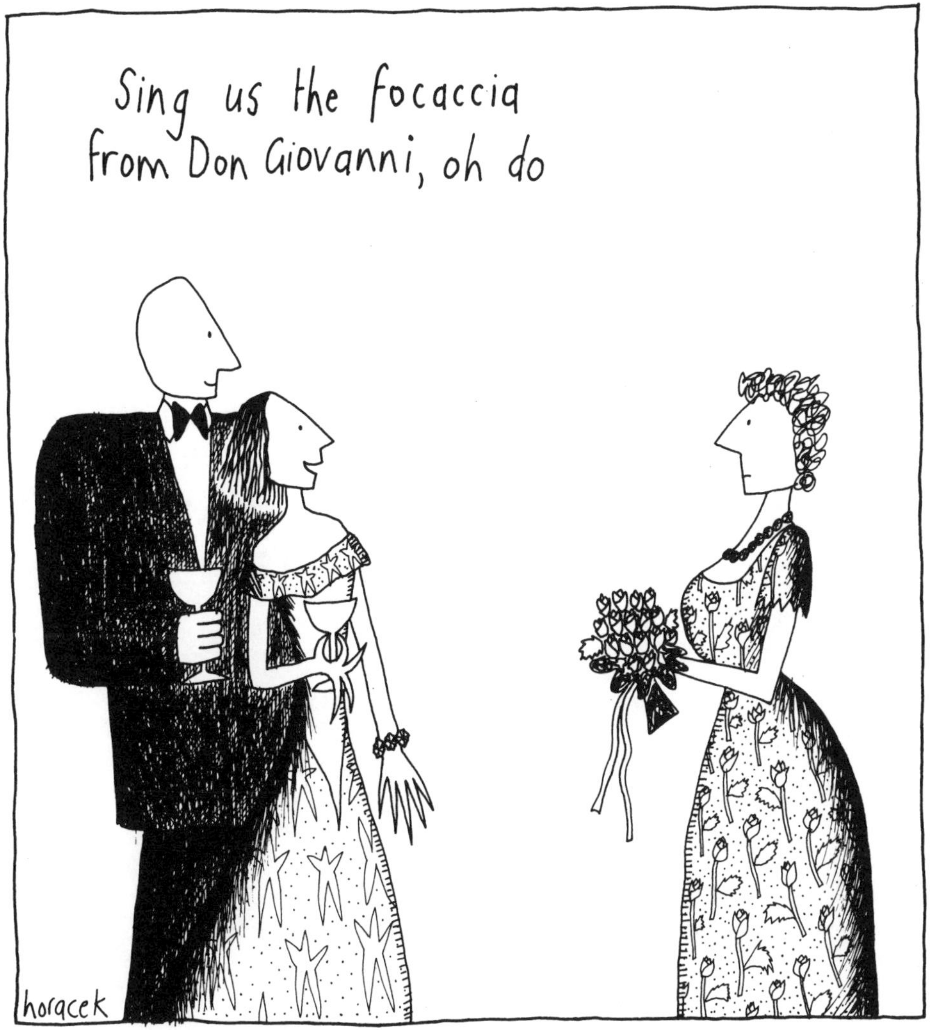
Sing us the focaccia
from Don Giovanni, oh do
horacek

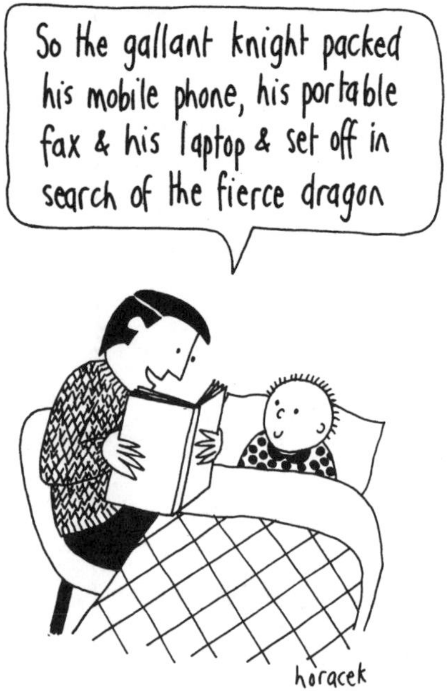
So the gallant knight packed his mobile phone, his portable fax & his laptop & set off in search of the fierce dragon
horacek

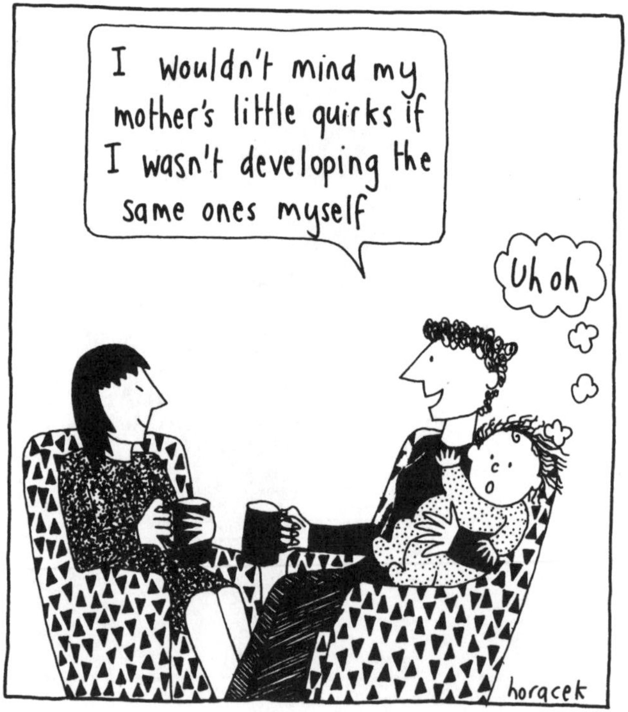
I wouldn't mind my mother's little quirks if I wasn't developing the same ones myself
Uh oh
horacek

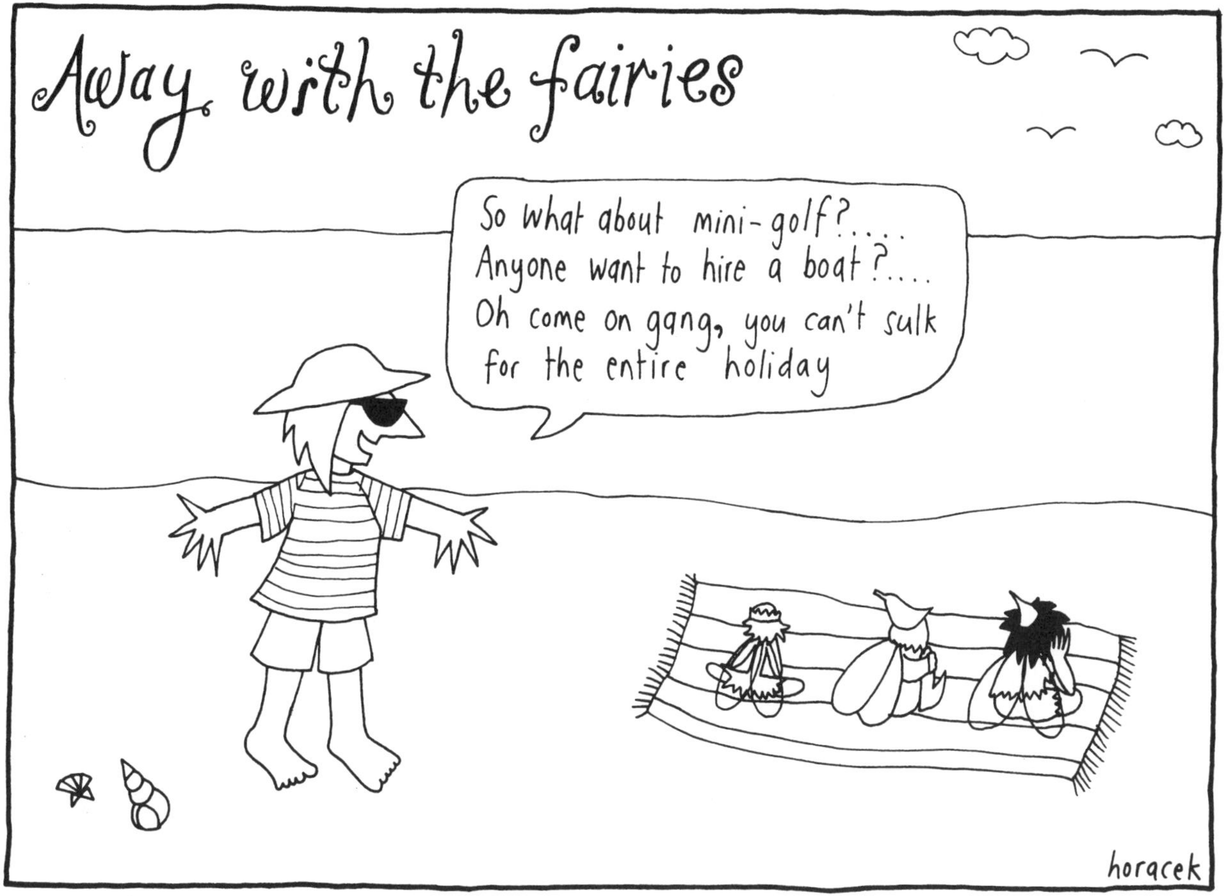
Away with the fairies
So what about mini-golf?....
Anyone want to hire a boat?....
Oh come on gang, you can't sulk for the entire holiday
horacek

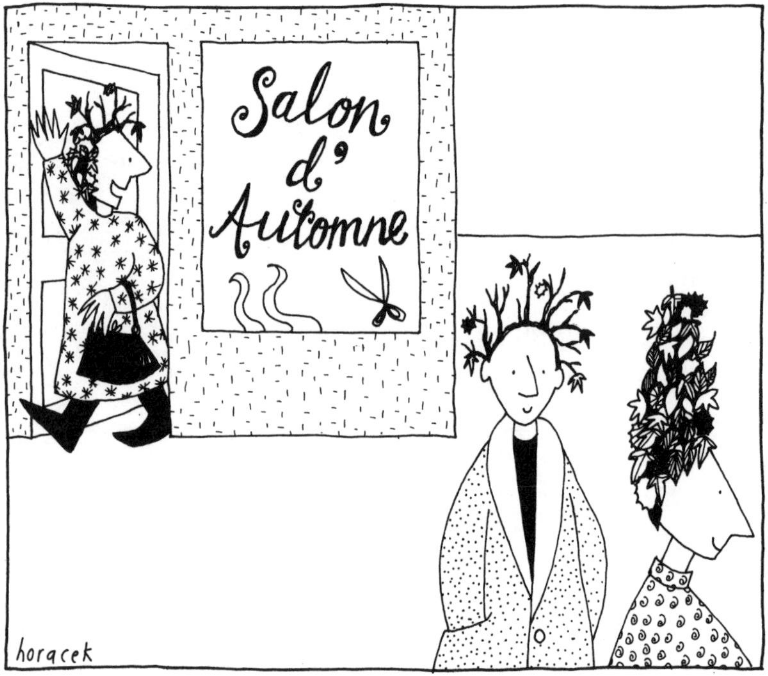
Salon d' Automne
horacek

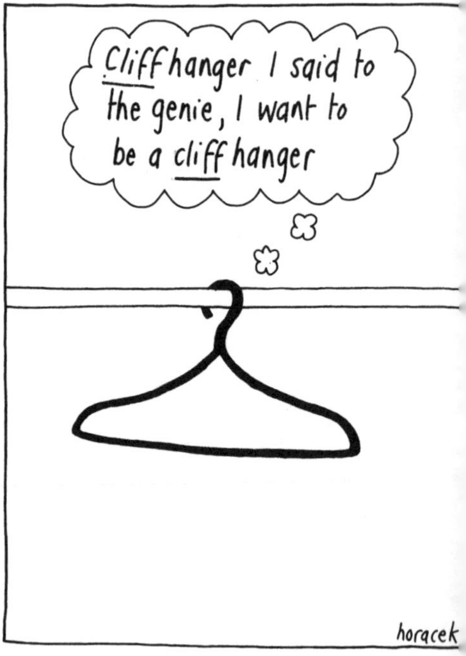
Cliff hanger I said to the genie, I want to be a cliff hanger
horacek

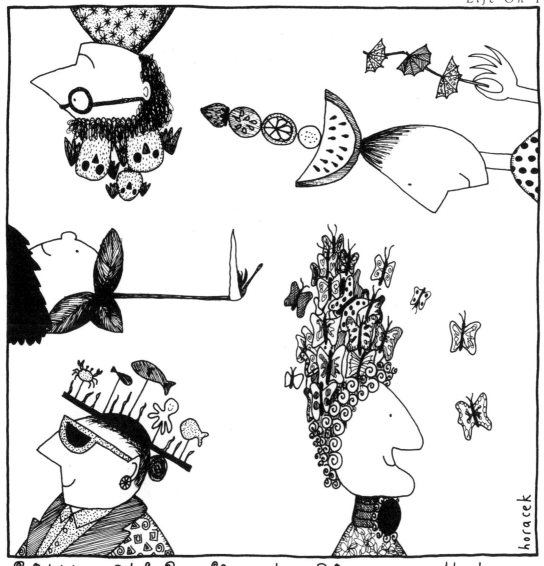

Little Old Ladies In Bizarre Hats

horacek

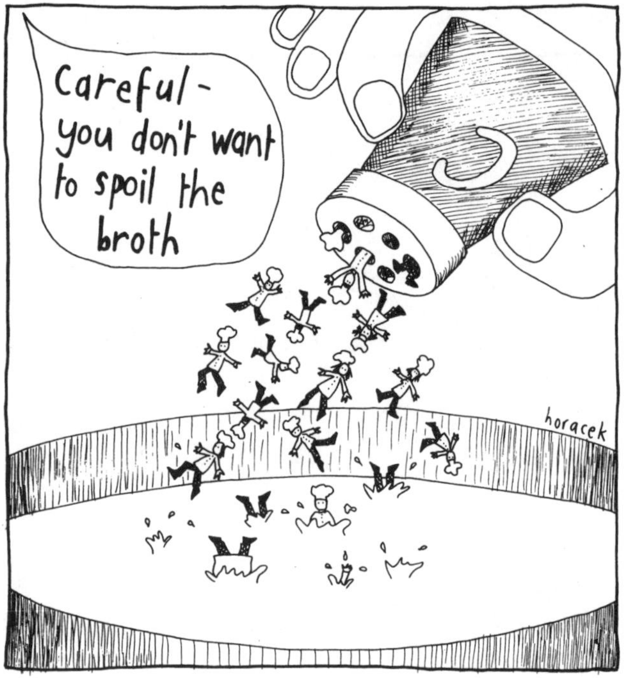
Careful - you don't want to spoil the broth
horacek

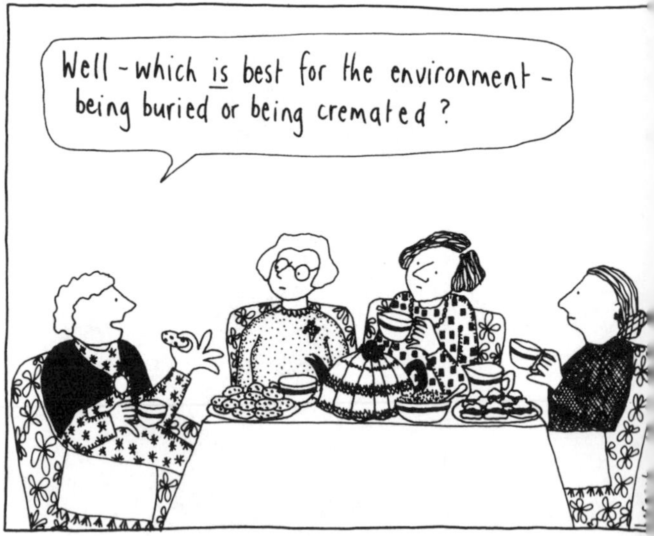
Well - which is best for the environment - being buried or being cremated ?

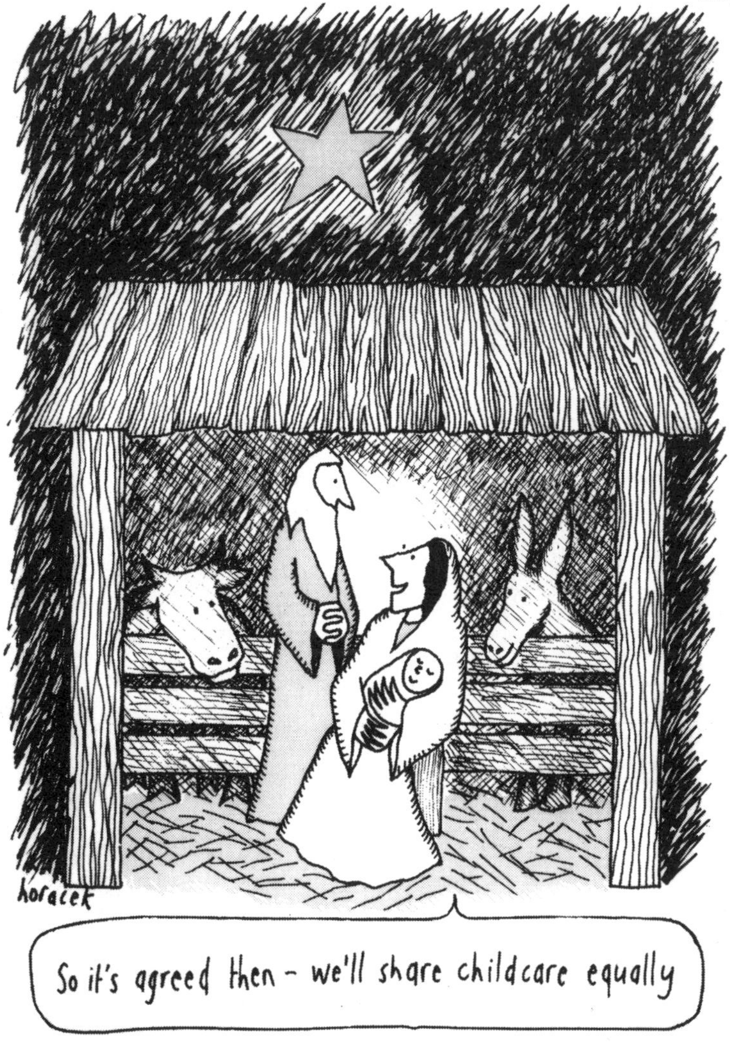
horacek
So it's agreed then - we'll share childcare equally

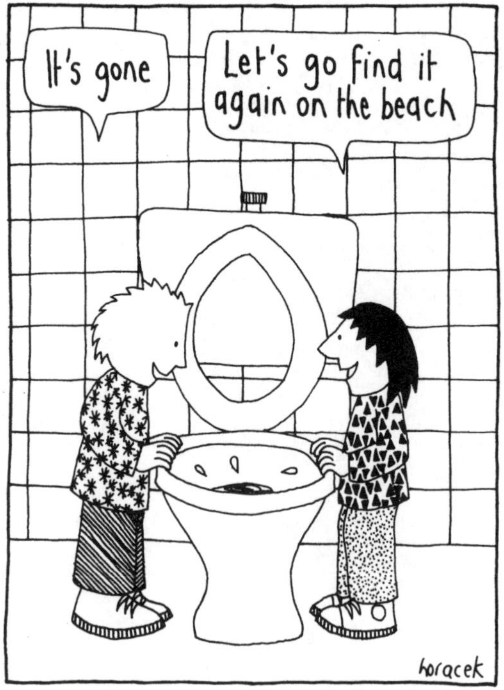
It's gone
Let's go find it again on the beach
horacek

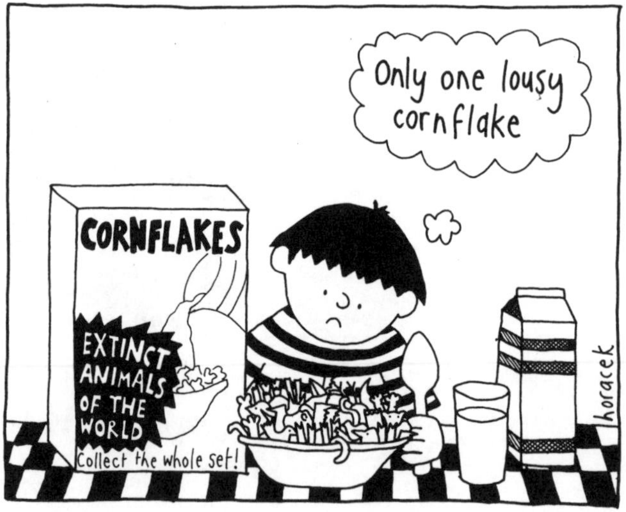
Only one lousy cornflake
CORNFLAKES
EXTINCT ANIMALS OF THE WORLD
Collect the whole set!
horacek

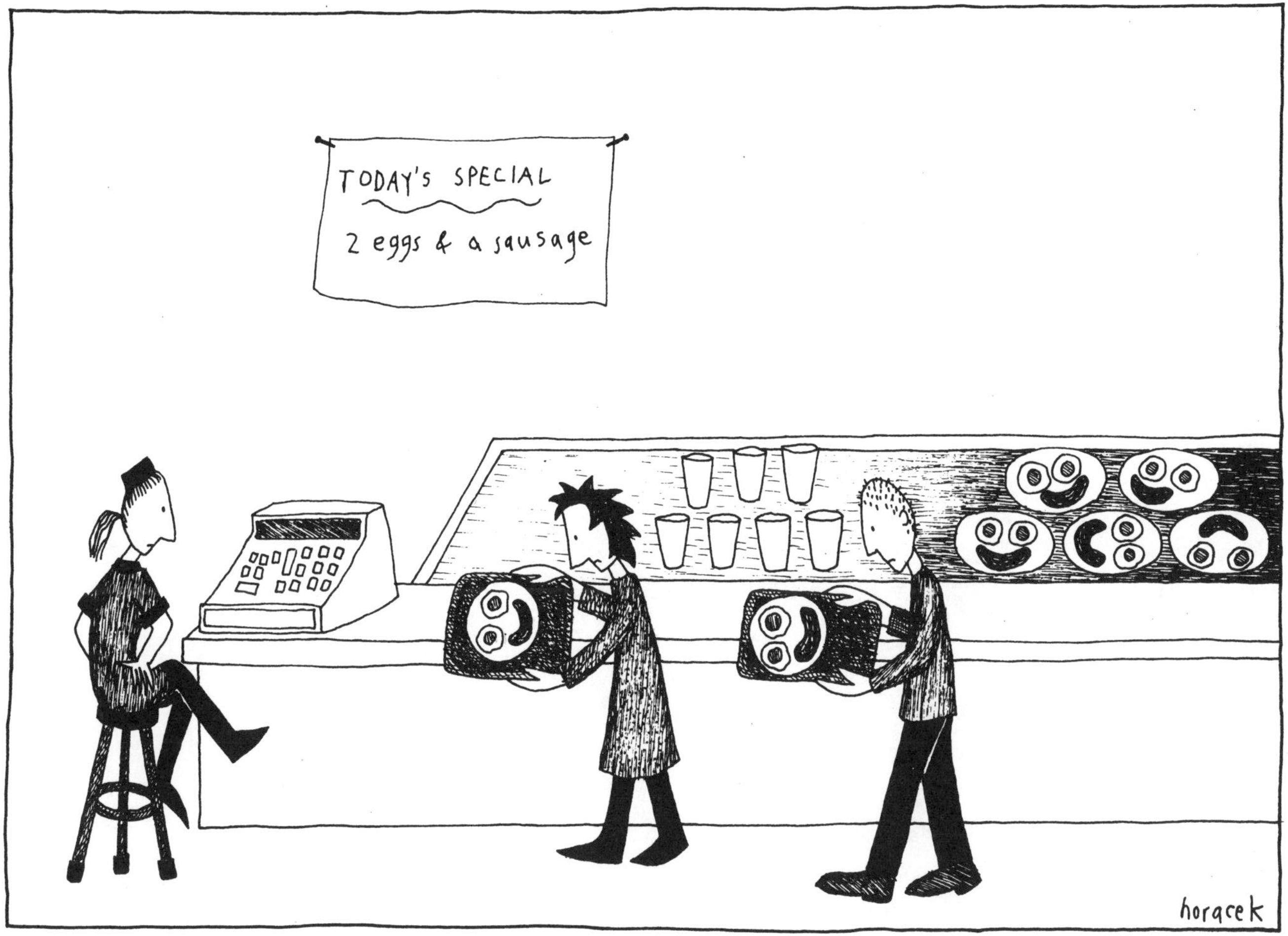
TODAY'S SPECIAL
2 eggs & a sausage
horacek

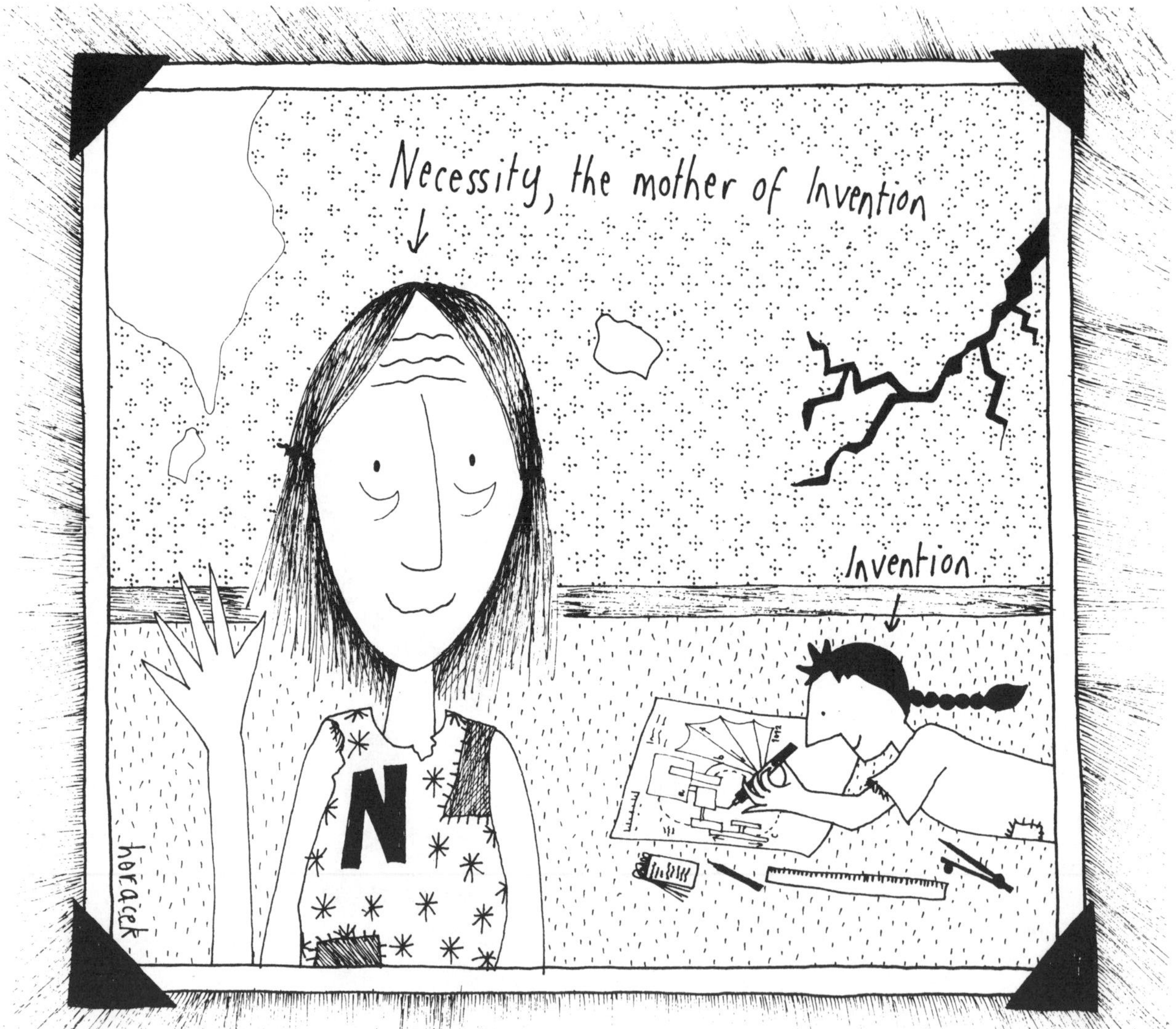
Necessity, the mother of Invention
Invention
horacek

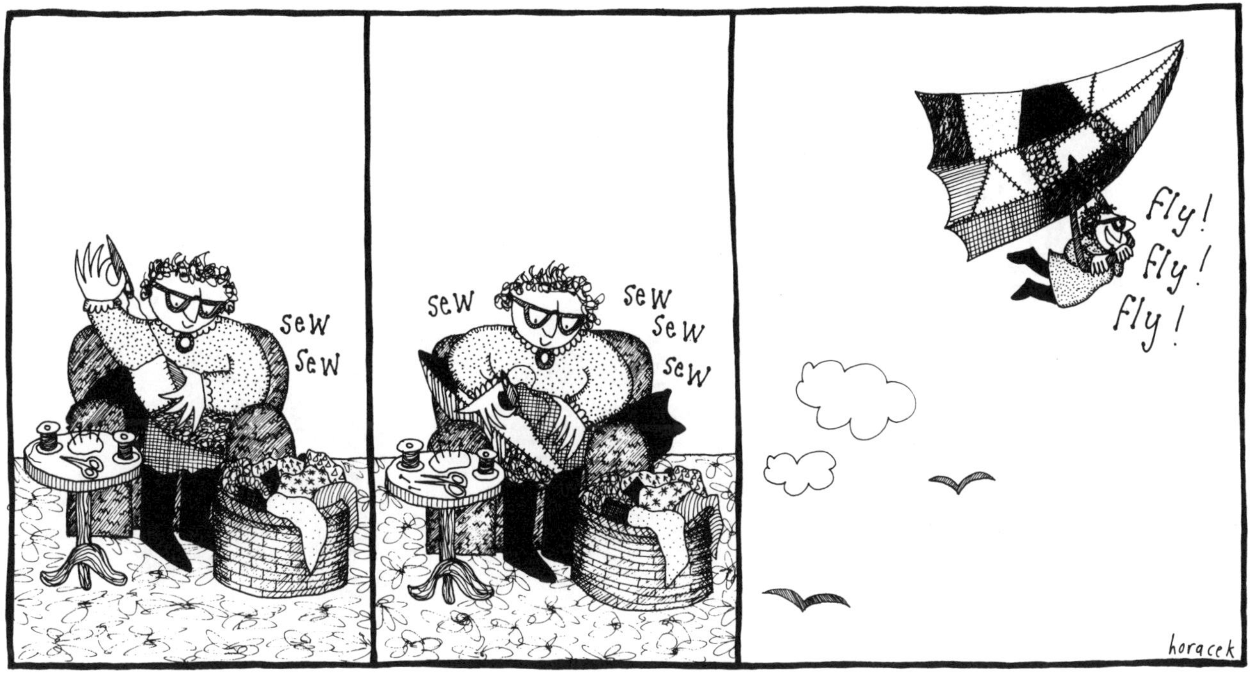
sew
sew
sew
sew
sew
sew
Fly!
Fly!
Fly!
horacek

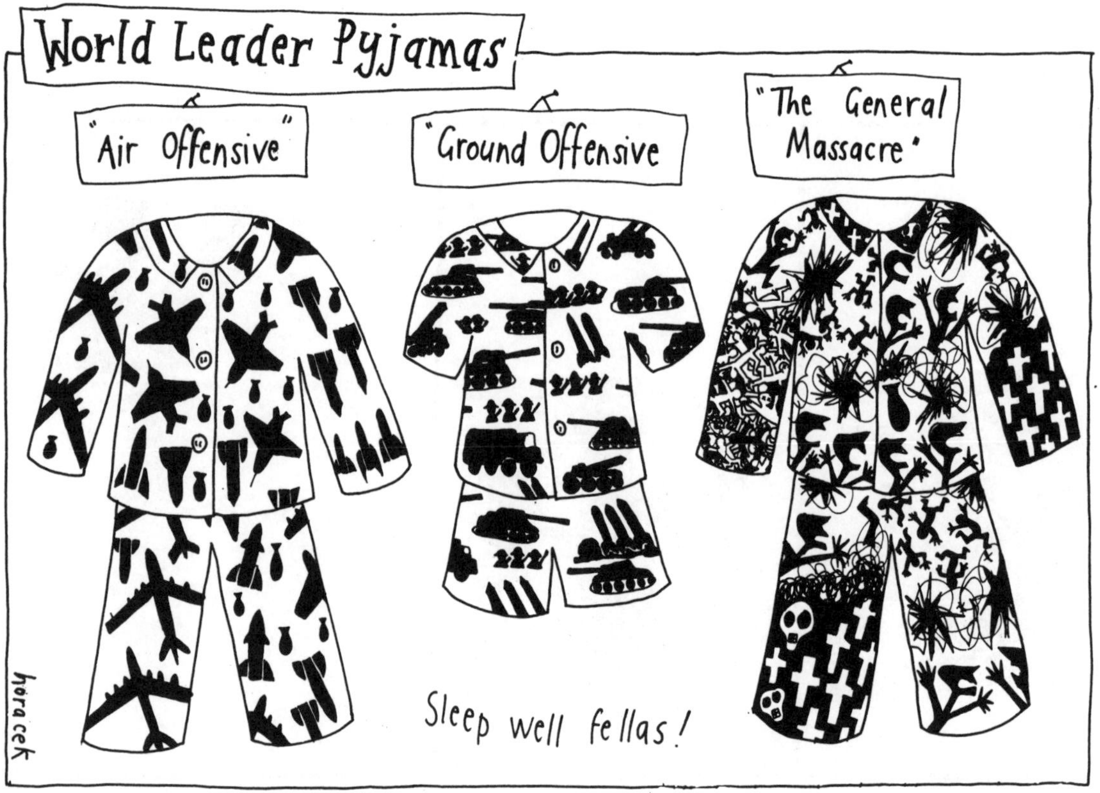
World Leader Pyjamas
"Air Offensive"
"Ground Offensive"
"The General Massacre"
Sleep well fellas!
horacek

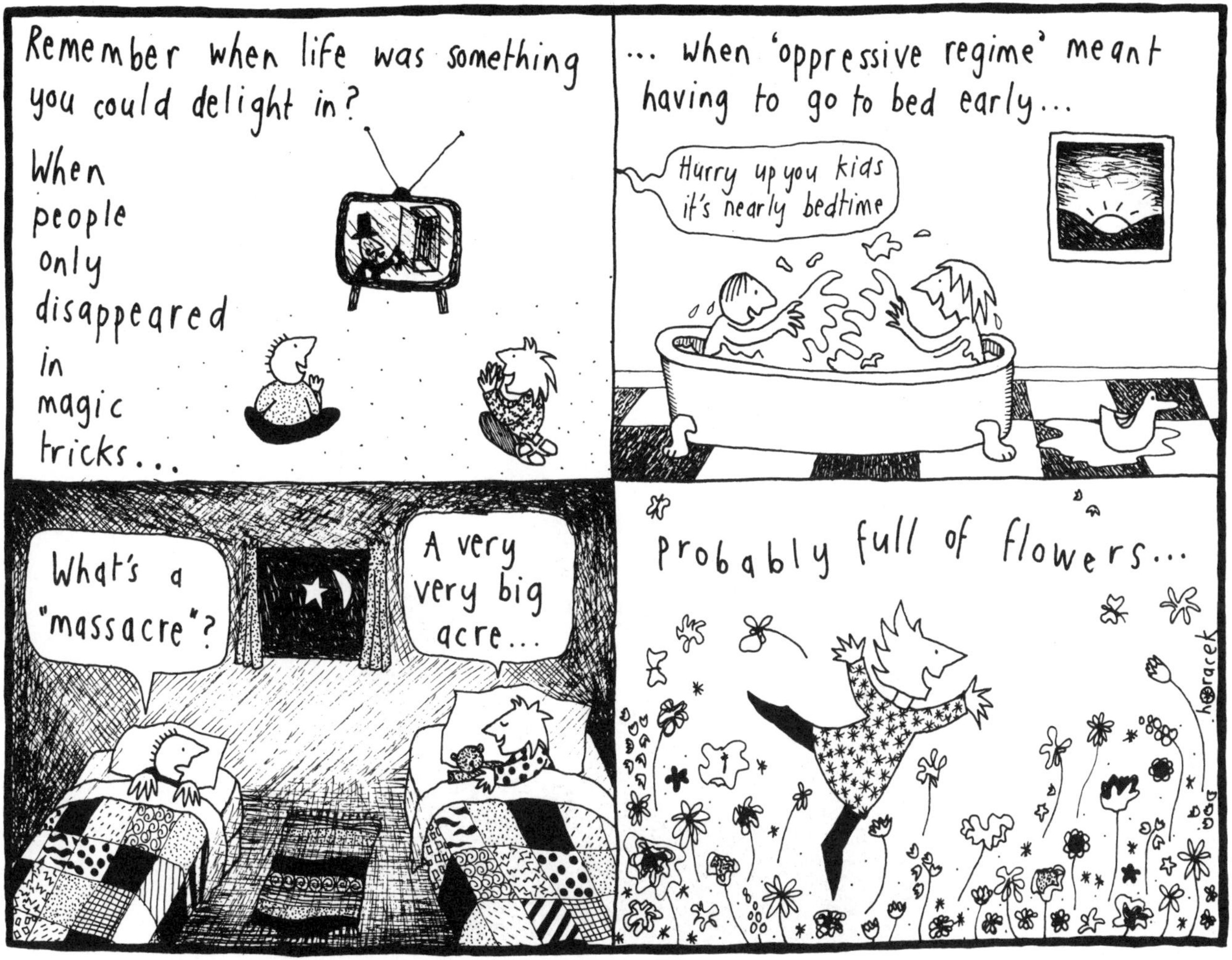
Remember when life was something you could delight in?
When people only disappeared in magic tricks...
... when 'oppressive regime' meant having to go to bed early...
Hurry up you kids it's nearly bedtime
What's a "massacre"?
A very very big acre...
probably full of flowers...
horacek

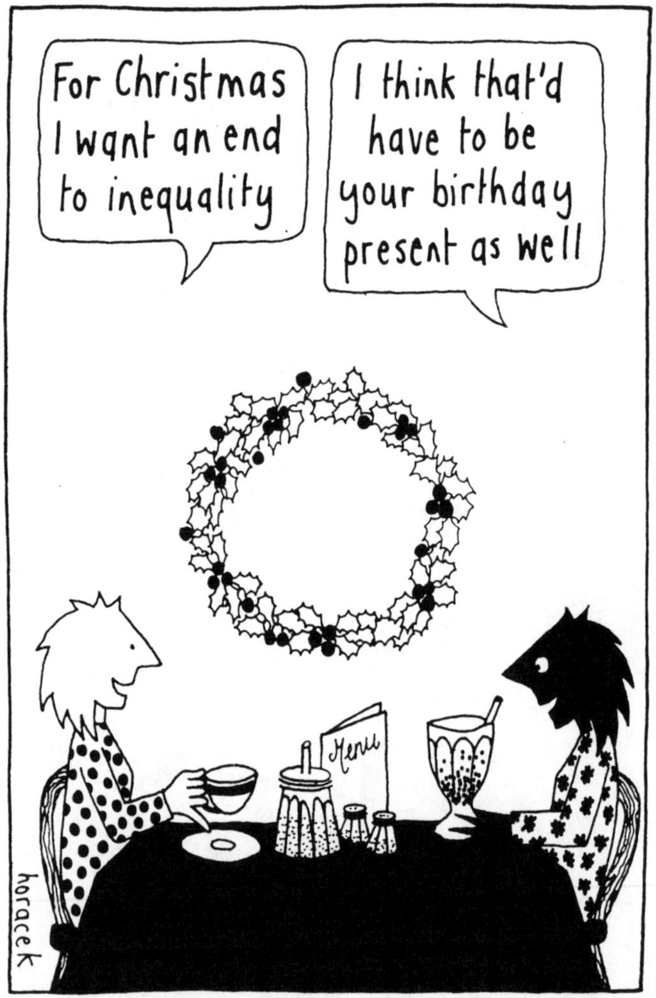
For Christmas I want an end to inequality
I think that'd have to be your birthday present as well
Menu
horacek

Afterword

It's been over a decade since *Life on the Edge* was first published. It was my first collection of cartoons, and consists of the best of the cartoons that I did in my first six or so years as a cartoonist. I am very proud of this book. I know it's not really the done thing to announce that you are proud of something you've been responsible for, but many of the cartoons here still make me laugh, all these years later, which I think is something to celebrate. A number of them are 'classics' in a way, cartoons where I think I've managed to perfectly hit issues on the head, especially fundamental issues for women like the double shift of working mothers, the way women's voices are (not) heard, violence against women, assumptions made on the basis of gender. Some of these I will probably never capture as succinctly or effectively again, try as I might. Cartoons such as 'Animal Impersonations', 'Dr Jekyll and Mrs Hyde', 'Prejudice Workshop', the 'Sharing Childcare Nativity' and 'Out alone wearing a provocative gender' have been republished many times, in places ranging from the densest academic textbooks to photocopied community group newsletters and everything in between. These are cartoons I feel I know like members of my family. There are also cartoons in this book that I don't come across so often. Seeing them again sometimes it's as if they were done by someone else and they are a lovely surprise.

The cartoons in this book mark my discovery of cartooning in my mid-twenties, which very importantly coincided with my discovery of feminism and politics in general. I decided to be a cartoonist because I realised that I wanted to give some sort of voice to things I felt about the world, and to speak up about things I believed were wrong. Cartooning was the ideal medium for what I wanted to say – able to convey very complicated messages in a simple fashion, and using humour to draw people in. Its directness not only had great appeal to me, it provided the perfect way to represent what I see as commonsense principles – that women should be treated equally, that the environment needs to be protected, that social justice is an essential goal, and so on.

I am often asked how I became a cartoonist. The answer is that I just drew some cartoons and started calling myself one. There aren't any formal cartoonist qualifications or courses you can do, it's the kind of thing you learn by doing. (By the way, if you're trying this at home, don't only concentrate on developing a drawing style, developing your ideas is at least as important, if not more so.) After I decided to become a cartoonist I put together a folio of my cartoons and went doorknocking, asking for cartoon work and gradually getting little bits and pieces. Not knocking on any old doors, but on select doors of groups and publications whose general principles I felt I shared – independent and left wing magazines and literary journals, community groups and women's groups. I started getting cartoons published here and there and the more my work appeared, the more I was asked to do.

Packaging messages in humour makes them very effective and cartooning is a wonderful political tool. Obviously as a form of political action, cartooning is a fairly safe option and Australia is a relatively safe place to do it, but for myself it's the best way I've found of making an individual contribution. Not that it absolves me from the responsibility of going to rallies, writing letters to politicians and donating money to campaigns and lots more. But it does mean that my working hours are to some extent also spent on the fight for goodness and light – trying to think of ways to question things, to highlight inequities, to make people think. And on very good days being able to catch glimpses of how the world could be a better place. I am full of admiration for those who devote their lives to working directly for social change and against injustices, such as the people currently working on behalf of those who come to Australia seeking refuge and asylum and instead receive interminable imprisonment. And I salute all cartoonists, artists and writers who create their work in places where they can be jailed for their beliefs. I wonder if I would be able to find the courage to speak out if I were in fear of my life.

When I started cartooning things were much simpler in many ways. Of course I was younger which automatically means things seem much simpler, far more black and white (which is obviously perfect for a black and white artist). But it isn't just me that's changed, society has too. Feminism has succeeded in getting women's issues onto the mainstream political agenda. Many battles have been won and there have been huge changes in legislation and in attitudes, and things are demonstrably better for many women. There may still be some mutterings that women shouldn't be educated, that they shouldn't work and that they should be at home in the kitchen, but these things are no longer widely accepted as fact by the general population. But things have also become more complicated and nowadays it is harder to identify a specific enemy, or even sometimes to work out what it would take to improve things. Violence against women hasn't gone away, nor have all the economic inequalities been addressed, in spite of both these things being recognised for the most part as very wrong. And sadly it hasn't turned out that women bosses and managers and women politicians are automatically more just, nor do they necessarily treat other women more fairly. (This is not in any way an argument against affirmative action – true equality is women being free to do their jobs as well or as badly as anyone else.) There are now also many people who pay lip service to all kinds of egalitarian ideas while still functioning as if they themselves have superior rights and abilities. Invisible barriers are complex and a lot harder to fight against. Not to mention very much harder to depict in cartoons.

Nowadays my work is published more regularly in the mainstream media but much of my cartooning career, including nearly all the cartoons in this book, has proudly taken place outside of this realm. I was a cartoonist for a long time before any of my work was published in any of the newspapers. Newspapers are a fantastic way to reach a large number of people in one fell swoop, but they aren't the only places where cartoons happen. The acknowledgements page of this book attests to the enormous variety of places where my cartoons were first published, and the cartoons were about a correspondingly large number of issues. I think it was the best apprenticeship I could have had.

A perennial difficulty for a freelance cartoonist is in getting your work out there (oh okay, that and trying to earn a living wage). The value of a cartoon is in it being seen by as many people as possible, that's what gives a cartoon life. I have always tried to find alternative methods of getting my work 'published', such as producing greeting cards and licensing other merchandise and more recently running a website. I discovered early on that you can't wait for external permission to do your work, for someone to invite you to contribute, you have to find ways to do it yourself.

I began making greeting cards in 1991 in response to a number of people complaining to me that there were no feminist Christmas cards available. I've been making greeting cards ever since, although I have to confess that I think I've run out of ideas for specifically feminist cartoons about Christmas. I've realised that producing cards is a fantastic method of putting cartoons out into the world. Cards are a wonderful way for cartoons to come into people's lives, one not subject to the vagaries of an editor, nor to the current preference of many newspapers and magazines for words over cartoons, or for neutral photographs over cute – but opinionated – drawings. There is also something very lovely about the fact that by being on a card a cartoon is turned into a message, into something that is passed on and shared, not just chuckled at by yourself. My cartoons now also appear on tea-towels, aprons and T-shirts. I love the irony that someone who often calls herself a feminist cartoonist has her work appearing on tea-towels and aprons.

The phenomenon that is the Internet has come about since *Life on the Edge* was first published. I worry about the gap that is being created between the technology rich and the technology poor, and the abysmal or dangerous quality of much of the information on the web. Nonetheless, there is something amazing about being able to be in touch with people all over the world, and to do it without the permission or control of any bureaucracy or media baron or publishing empire. And as what the powers-that-be choose to publish becomes more and more narrow, it's fantastic to have the Internet as a partial antidote. A few years ago when I was 'between jobs' for a long time and my work wasn't really appearing anywhere, I decided to introduce a Topic of the Month to my website. Every month I gather twelve to twenty cartoons I've done on a certain topic and post them onto my website, then send an email to my mailing list telling everyone what this month's topic is. Topics so far have included Feminism (of course), Fish, Love, Computers, Mornings, No War and lots more. (If you'd like to join the mailing list, send an email to newsletter@horacek.com.au with the word 'subscribe' as the subject. It's free.) I don't think the audience for anything that isn't on television is ever going to be huge, but my mailing list continues to slowly grow. Through it I am in touch with people all over the world who are interested in my work, a self-selected audience that is very dear to me.

Over the years I've wondered a lot if cartoons can ever change anything. I've often said that I became a cartoonist to try and change the world but in fact many of the ways in which the world has changed over the last decade have been for the worse. And are my cartoons only preaching to the converted anyway? (Not that there's anything wrong with that *per se* – as has often been said, the converted need temples to pray in too.) But I do think that there is something about doing work relating to women's experience that is of immense value. It is putting forward a speaking position that has so often either not been heard or has been dismissed as not important. It creates places in which women can recognise ourselves and our own lives, and our shared experience. Not that I would ever claim to speak for all women and I am also very aware that, while the position of women generally is devalued, I have had a life of incredible privilege compared to the bulk of the world's population, having had the luck to be born white and middle class in a wealthy developed nation. (Luckily I've had to cope with being left-handed in a right-handed world or I wouldn't feel that I could create anything at all.)

My current answer is that I don't think cartoons alone can change anything. But I think the more voices raised in dissent the more likely there is to be change. And the more that women's experience and the experience of being women is recognised as equally important as that of men's, the more likely it is that women will be encouraged to be effective in their own areas. And the more we question injustice and unsustainable practices everywhere, and try to bring governments and business to account, then the better off we'll be.

Maybe that's all too hopelessly idealistic for this world in the early days of the new millennium with its creeping conservatism and intransigence. Perhaps I should just limit myself to a version of the Hippocratic oath that doctors used to take "If you can do no good, at least do no harm" with this bit added "And for goodness sake try to make them laugh."

For the record, I don't think there's anything wrong with cartoons that are simply jokes. I do lots of cartoons that are just plain silly, more and more of them it seems as life becomes increasingly complicated. Of course, women are always the main characters, so most of the cartoons do still contain a slight challenge to the status quo (surprisingly even in 2003, women as main characters *IS* still a challenge to the status quo). But silly for silly's sake is a healthy way to go too.

At the launch of *Life on the Edge* in 1992 I said that 'As my work has become better known, I meet people who say "You're Judy Horacek, you're in our toilet".' At the time I said that I hadn't yet worked out the appropriate response, and eleven years later I still haven't. But as all cartoonists know, there is no higher accolade than having a cartoon touch someone so that they want to look at it for more than the few seconds that it takes to get the joke, that they want to be able to return to it and what it says. I've never written an Afterword before, but it seems an appropriate place to say thank you to all the people who have supported my work over the years since I first became a cartoonist and since this book first came out. Thank you to those people who have published my cartoons and given me work, and especially thank you to all the people who have enjoyed the cartoons, to all the people who have told me how much a certain cartoon of mine means to them, and thanks to everyone who has laughed.

Judy Horacek, 2003

Other titles from Spinifex Press

ARTS AND CULTURE

If Passion Were a Flower ...

Lariane Fonseca

Inspired by the writing of Virginia Woolf and the painting of Georgia O'Keefe, Lariane Fonseca uses the camera to depict the "passion of flowers".

The gift book of choice for anniversaries or very special friends.

– Tee Corrinne, *Feminist Bookstore News*

ISBN 1-875559-06-X

Charts and Soundings: Some Small Navigational Aids

Sue Fitchett and Jane Zusters

[A] book of myths and a loaded camera . . . The combination of verbal and visual imagery resonates with connections. – Riemke Ensing

With twenty-two photographs by Jane Zusters and twenty poems by Sue Fitchett, this book illuminates the New Zealand landscape.

ISBN 0-473-06192-9

(Available from Spinifex in Australia)

Don't Shoot Darling: Women's Independent Filmmaking in Australia

Edited by Annette Blonski, Barbara Creed and Freda Freiberg

This book marks the triumphant, flowering of women's filmmaking, looking back to the initiatives of the '70s.　　　　　　　　　　　　　　　– Adrian Martin, *The Age*

ISBN 0-86436-058-4

Painting Myself In

Nina Mariette

Expressing oneself through creativity can be an immensely challenging and satisfying experience. Nina Mariette, a survivor of childhood abuse, uses painting to make sense of her past, and tells her story with pictures and words.

ISBN 1-875559-73-6

(Available from Spinifex in Australia)

INDIGENOUS ISSUES

Kick the Tin

Doris Kartinyeri

When Doris Kartinyeri was a month old, her mother died, and Doris was removed from the hospital and placed in Colebrook Home. A moving testimony from one of the Stolen Generation.

With a Foreword by Lowitja O'Donoghue, Doris Kartinyeri's story allows the reader to understand how it felt to be separated from family and from the Ngarrindjeri culture into which she had been born.

ISBN 1-875559-95-7

Ngarrindjeri Wurruwarrin: A world that is, was, and will be

Diane Bell

Winner, Gleebooks Award for Cultural or Literary Critique, NSW Premier's Awards

A magisterial work . . . every Ngarrindjeri person I have spoken to applauds this book. Ethnographies of this sort are usually avoided for any number of reasons, not the least of which is the sense that attempting such a study is too hard. That Bell attempts and succeeds in this without sacrificing scholarship or standards is a magnificent achievement.

– Christine Nicholls, *Times Higher Educational Supplement*

ISBN 1-875559-71-X

FICTION

Juggling Truths

Unity Dow

Unity Dow's novels are always more than just stories . . . and while her legal background informs her perception it does not weigh down her prose, which is vivid, lyrical and sometimes wickedly funny. — Juliette Hughes, *The Age*

ISBN 1-876756-38-1

Speak the Truth, Laughing

Rose Zwi

Shortlisted for the Steel Rudd Award
Human Rights Award Winning author

An accomplished collection which will find many appreciative readers.

— Deborah Stone, *Australian Jewish News*

ISBN 1-876756-21-7

If you would like to know more about Spinifex Press,
write for a free catalogue or visit our website

Spinifex Press

PO Box 212 North Melbourne

Victoria 3051 Australia

<http://www.spinifexpress.com.au>